Stories From Ordinary People
Who Created Extraordinary Lives

TOTAL LIFE
TRANSFORMATION

Turning Your Pain into Passion and Living on Purpose

KERRY B. FISHER
LAWRENCE TUAZON

TOTAL LIFE TRANSFORMATION:
TURNING YOUR PAIN INTO PASSION AND LIVING ON PURPOSE.
Copyright © 2023 by Kerry Fisher, Lawrence Tuazon

Disclaimer—The advice, guidelines, and all suggested material in this book is given in the spirit of information with no claims to any particular guaranteed outcomes. This book does not replace professional physical or mental support or counselling. Anyone deciding to add physical or mental exercises to their life should reach out to a licensed medical doctor or therapist before following any of the advice in this book. The authors, publishers, editors, distributors, and organizers do not assume and hereby disclaim any liability to any party for any loss, damage, or disruption caused by anything written in this book.

Library of Congress Cataloging-in-Publication Data
Names: Fisher, Kerry, Author; Lawrence Tuazon, Author
Title: *TOTAL LIFE TRANSFORMATION: TURNING YOUR PAIN INTO PASSION AND LIVING ON PURPOSE*

LCCN 2023916214

ISBN 978-1-958165-18-8 (hardback)
ISBN 978-1-958165-19-5 (paperback)
ISBN 978-1-958165-20-1 (eBook)

Nonfiction, Mind, Body & Spirit, Self-Help, Personal Development

Contents

Foreword

Have you ever had a time in life where you were totally thrown off balance? Perhaps it was triggered by a difficult event or a hard time in your life, a moment that dropped you to your knees. If so, you are not alone. We all have those 'dark moments of the soul' moments and they are very, very difficult. They are the times in life where we are struggling; we aren't sure who we are or why we are here. We doubt ourselves, we question everything, perhaps we wonder if we can even go on. Those moments are painful and while we are in them, we aren't sure we will ever be able to stand back up.

The good news is that in those moments, we have a choice. We can choose to stay down, or we can decide to get up and continue to soldier forward. When we choose to get back up, those dark moments of the soul can become times of great transformation. It is in our darkest times that huge growth can happen if we let it. If we decide to face our pain and begin to move forward, we can use those moments to catapult us to a new level. There is a saying, "What doesn't kill you makes you stronger," and it absolutely rings true.

In this book, you will find amazing stories of transformation. We have gathered stories from people from around the world to help you see that no matter where you are in life, you can change everything.The authors in this book have shared very honestly and vulnerably, detailing those moments when life knocked them down. They talk about the experiences which shaped them, but which also made them wonder if they could ever become the person they wanted to be. The stories are deeply compelling and remind us yet again, that every person's story is powerful and every story has lessons.

In each chapter, you will find a story about the author's life journey, one of the times when life dealt them a hard blow, when things weren't going well. The stories are incredible and will touch you deeply. The best part, however, is the way that each author shares their journey away from their pain. They detail the steps they took to create a life of purpose and meaning, how they turned the darkness into light.

This is a book of inspiration, but it is also a book where you can learn simple tools so that you, too, can make your way from where you are to where you want to go. In this way, the book is a manual for life. If you apply the tools, tips, and techniques that are detailed in each chapter, you too can change your life.

Get ready to be inspired! You will be absolutely swept away by the stories of courage shared here. It is our wish that these stories and the tools that each author shares will help you look at your life differently. That the stories will help you to know that you are not alone, that others have walked the path you are on now.

It is our greatest wish that you will realize that you can turn your pain into purpose and live the life of your dreams. We have done it and you can do it too. We are rooting for you!

With love,
Kerry and Lawrence

No, You Haven't

by Elyse Alexander

*Do not judge me by my success,
judge me by how many times I fell down
and got back up again.*

~Nelson Mandela

My Story

------ 🌺 ------

Since I suppressed it, it always remained just beneath the surface, bubbling and leaking out. I'm sharing this with you, hoping you won't repeat my mistakes. Life, I've learned, often makes us repeat errors until we grasp the lesson. I know I certainly did. I am sharing my story with you to show that regardless of where you are, you can shape a different, better life. I achieved it, and you can too.

Sit tight, and I'll narrate how I became the princess of a little town called Bel Air.

Dialing with trembling fingers while seated at the library's window sill. A woman answers, inquiring my name and the reason for my call. With a gulp, I utter, "I need an appointment for an abortion." I remember how those words clung like cherry cough syrup. She wasn't my first call that day; I had to contact multiple offices. The first time I needed to persistently seek aid until I received it.

It's in such pivotal life moments that you decide whether to remain the same or transform. These moments can also trigger you and open up an old wound. That was my experience then. I unearthed a childhood wound; the memory of my mother urging me not to have kids young like she did, fearing I'd repeat her "mistakes." In that instant, I felt like I'd let her down, a failure in life. This thought ignited a chain reaction, questioning my predispositions.

In a blink, I was transported back to a vivid memory that shaped my identity. Facing that little girl, I see and hear her distinctly, embodying her perspective. Looking at her in the walk-in closet near the safe, gripped by fear, the memory endured. Witnessing her struggle to soothe her uncontrollable mother and herself. You can't give what you lack, perpetuating the cycle.

Unaware of the extent of inherited anxiety, I delved deeper, realizing I felt unworthy. I assumed these matters were resolved, but unaddressed issues resurface relentlessly. Deep-seated ancestral patterns endure within us. Some might not even be our own; we pick them up like extra baggage. Patterns we thought we'd outgrown reemerge with vigor. Because we haven't forgiven ourselves enough, haven't shown ourselves sufficient love.

Can we truly heal generations-old trauma in mere days? Those pathways are deeply etched; we can't erase them overnight.

Don't be spiritually naive; I found myself there for years. Accept that you're your harshest critic, beating yourself before others can.

Why can't I grasp the lesson of getting out of my own way? As children, we expect our parents to be flawless, knowing everything. Growing up, reality reveals their imperfections. It alters your perception of yourself.

Emerging from anesthesia, disoriented but recalling each detail, I needed assistance. I'd taken myself as far as possible; I had to prioritize my well-being to survive. This wouldn't fade with time. For the first time, I sought help beyond myself, after futile solo attempts.

I couldn't mend my life or choices solo; I felt more helpless than when I was the "nice girl." Unbelievably, asking for help seemed daunting. I feared they wouldn't aid me, or worse, judge my decisions. I'd already disqualified them mentally before asking. I had to lean on others for my needs, uncomfortable but necessary. My belief that if you can't do something alone, you're not meant for it shattered. I was wrong. My discomfort led to tearful nights.

Seeking help for the clinic visit was necessary. Being far along, I had to travel across town to a special facility. Sharing this story was once daunting due to shame. Maybe your experience differs, but you've faced challenges that unveiled your strength. We forget how strong we are when life gets too close.

Asking for assistance to enter bed, facing the unknown, was humbling. I questioned whether I could manage alone. I recall every color of the wallpaper, the excruciating pain, and my determination to endure. Discovering inner strength, self-love, and resilience. You're capable of more than you fathom. Pain compels until a vision beckons.

Guarding such a colossal secret wasn't new. I questioned if he was worthy of being the father of my children. It hit me hard; he wasn't who I needed. I realized I didn't need him. I'd managed this journey alone. A powerful moment that now moves me to tears. I was strong all along. Instances like these shattered my self-worth, yet patterns persisted.

Taking a single day off classes was my limit, not wanting questions. An old pattern of neglecting self-care arose. A huge event, my college graduation, was days away. We prepared a five-course themed meal, a yearly final. I hid my turmoil, while others reveled. I played the role of the good girl, masking my pain.

Underneath my exterior, I was furious at myself, him, the situation. I carried a smile, masking the turmoil. Opening up to my first soul sister was rare. Vulnerability demands courage. Alyssa proved one person can see what you can't. I exposed my vulnerabilities, then braced for disappointment.

The anesthesia-triggered memory had marked me. Facing my trauma, I understood that the trauma spanned generations. It called for healing. The journey is endless, a priority from the start. Make time daily and weekly for profound healing. Push yourself to grow, even in discomfort. Ho'oponopono, Hawaiian meditation, started reshaping my path.

Ho'oponopono held space for healing. Words—love, sorry, forgive me, thank you—transmuted fear into love. It shortened the path to self-love, diminishing triggers. Connecting with my inner child, guiding her, nurturing healing. The journey is continuous, requiring consistency. Discover tools that resonate; uniqueness matters.

I started participating in online calls focused on Ho'oponopono. My connection with the divine grew. Forgiveness became transformative. The past doesn't dictate the future. Unearth your potential. I peeled layers, knowing healing required patience. Ho'oponopono gave roots, aiding growth independently.

Healing demands consistent effort. Prioritize healing early, committing to daily and weekly practice. Discover your unique way to stay consistent. Remind yourself of your strength. The healing path continues, prompting self-discovery. You are more powerful than you realize; remember your strength.

The Ho'oponopono Meditation

Come into a comfortable seated position. Relax deeply. Close your eyes. Begin to repeat these phrases:

- I'm sorry
- Please forgive me

- Thank you
- I love you

Continue repeating these phrases and see if any person comes into your mind. If so, you might want to direct the phrases towards the vision of that person. You can also expand and personalize the meditation if you would like by adding to each phrase. Here's an example using a fictitious Joe. You can use this format but feel free to tailor this to work for you.

- I'm sorry for hurting you Joe.
- Please forgive me for not being there for you.
- Thank you Joe
- I love you Joe.

You can use this as a general prayer, with no intended recipient or you can tailor it to the exact person you would like to gain forgiveness from. And don't forget, you can use this prayer towards yourself, to give yourself the well deserved love and forgiveness and gratitude you deserve.

Please feel free to reach out to me if you would like more information on this meditation or if you need any guidance as you navigate the difficult times in your life. I look forward to connecting.

Sending you love,
Elyce

About the Author

Elyse Alexander is a Wealth Mindset Business Coach who helps female dreamers overcome mediocrity so they can have freedom of their mind + money.

After going from Chocolatier to Wealth Mindset Business Coach, Elyse uses her experience to help others create sustainable financial freedom and self-mastery to reach their potential faster. She has years of experience working with those who have tried everything to gain financial freedom and feel like NOTHING works for them. By addressing the source of their wealth blocks, Elyse breaks through experiences from the inside out, allowing her clients to create wealth differently so they can Quantum Leap more quickly into Quantum Worth.

Elyse is the creator of Burning Pure Community, where she mentors entrepreneurs to their BEST Life of financial freedom. She is the author of the upcoming book "Nice girls don't."

She has spoken about Getting in the room, Wealth creation, Fear of success, Community, Mindset, Perfectionism, and Imposter Syndrome on numerous stages including regularly on her own Mindvalley live events series. She's also been featured on the Claim Your Worth Podcast with Darcey Elizabeth and published in 4.20 media.

Author Contact Information

Email: enalexander94@gmail.com

The Double-Edged Sword We Call Love

by Faraaz Ali

We are all born with the capacity to love;
it's our willingness to love
that is a choice that defines how we want to live life.

~Faraaz Ali

ove has been a constant presence throughout human history, with the power to unite or divide, bring pleasure or pain, expand or contract the soul, and create or destroy life. Its effects on humans can be positive or negative, raising the question of whether we should have been taught about it more extensively in school.

In my opinion, the answer is a definite yes! Emotional regulation, love psychology, and relational intelligence are essential tools that can help us to avoid heartbreak and teach us how to foster love from within. This chapter will introduce lessons to help individuals utilize love as a tool for greatness and a higher purpose.

This chapter will not dwell on my personal breakup pain from past relationships, but rather provide a collective summary of what I have learned and how to deal with love more efficiently. Anyone curious about the breakup events, here is the short summary. It involved tears, ice cream, other emotionally triggered junk food, and a whole lot of victim mindset manifestation for two to three intense weeks, followed by a few months of disliking love songs and the "I can't trust the world vibes."

The lessons I'm about to share are what I wish I could have given my younger self to bounce back from breakups more effectively or, ideally, prevent them from happening. But before we introduce the strategies for personal growth, let's first explore the concept of love.

What is Love?

If you remember that song, go ahead and sing it, baby. Loud and proud. We often describe love as an emotion, feeling, or state of being rather than a form of energy in the traditional scientific sense. While there are undoubtedly energetic components involved in the experience of love (such as the release of hormones like oxytocin and dopamine), love is typically not thought of as a type of energy like heat, light, or electricity.

Despite the science, some people use the concept of "love energy" or "positive energy" to describe the positive feelings and emotions associated with love and the sense of connection and unity that can come from loving relationships. However, this is more of a symbolic or spiritual interpretation of love rather than a scientific one. In general, the nature of love is complex and multifaceted, and it can be challenging to capture or describe it using any framework or language entirely.

The psychology of falling in love is a fascinating subject studied extensively by researchers. When we fall in love, our brains undergo significant changes that can affect our behavior and emotions. For example, releasing dopamine and other neurochemicals can create euphoria and pleasure, motivating us to pursue our romantic interests. Additionally, falling in love can activate brain regions associated with reward, empathy, and social cognition. This activation can lead to heightened intimacy, trust, and connection with our partner or partners. On the other hand, falling out of love can involve:

- A reversal of some of these processes.
- Detachment.
- Leading to feelings of loneliness.
- Even physical pain.

Overall, understanding the psychology of falling in and out of love can help us make sense of our own experiences and emotions, and navigate the ups and downs of romantic relationships more effectively.

Falling in Love

Remember the first time you looked at that one person; they took your breath away. Nothing else mattered in the present moment. What you desired is what you saw, and what you saw was right in front of you. This feeling was my story from high school to university and beyond. This experience is often confused as love, but it is rather lust. My young heart did not know the difference, and was falling in love multiple times a week.

Lesson 1:
Know the Difference Between Love and Lust

Love and lust are often confused and used interchangeably, but they are distinct experiences with different emotional and physical components.

Love is a deep and emotional connection that develops over time. It involves a sense of mutual respect, trust, and commitment between two people. Love's sole focus is not on physical attraction or sexual desire, but rather encompasses a broad range of emotions, including compassion, empathy, and selflessness.

Lust, on the other hand, is primarily driven by physical attraction and sexual desire. It can be intense and immediate, but it does not involve the emotional intimacy and depth of love. Lust can be fleeting, and often dissipates once the physical attraction wanes or is fulfilled. Love and lust also have different effects on our behavior and relationships. Love builds solid and lasting connections, while lust often leads to casual encounters or short-term flings. Love encourages us to prioritize the well-being of our partner, while lust can lead to more selfish and impulsive actions.

While love and lust can be essential aspects of romantic relationships, it is crucial to understand their differences to avoid confusion or disappointment. Building a solid foundation of love requires trust and emotional intimacy. These two elements are essential for developing healthy, fulfilling relationships that stand the test of time.

Looking back, I wish I had understood the differences between love and lust when I entered the dating world. In my teenage years, I would seek out physically attractive partners without considering the importance of a deeper emotional connection. Unfortunately, this pattern of behavior ultimately led to heartbreak.

As young lovers, we often become deeply invested in our relationships, but the end result can be painful if our attraction is rooted in lust rather than love. Being vulnerable, having all walls down, and leaving my heart and mind open allowed me to receive and connect. At this stage, I convinced myself that my partner was "the one" for me, planning our future with thoughts of marriage, children, world travel, and other shared experiences. This level of thinking was after three months in a relationship. Seriously, what was I thinking?

However, my motivations arose primarily from sexual desires. Secondary was the need for companionship and validation. My relationships didn't have the foundation to last. Looking back, I realize that while I was between sixteen and twenty years old, I focused on satisfying my ego and physical desires, with only a tiny percentage of my motivation coming from a genuine connection with my partner. I needed to focus on self-love as my initial solution to ensure I operated from a place of love. Lust was in the driver's seat. The hormones pushed love to the backseat passenger status.

Lesson 2:
Learn to Love Yourself First

Opening your heart, being vulnerable, and investing all of yourself in a relationship to later find out you made a misjudgement is a challenging place to find yourself. You feel betrayed, let down, and emotionally wounded, and to add to that, your reduced sexual intimacy can get you feeling edgy.

That dopamine and oxytocin hit you get from a partner is missed tremendously. It makes me wonder, when I used to tell girls back then, "I missed you," what did I mean? This statement was very surface level, as my inner desires said, "I miss being with you, your kiss, your touch, making love to you, and how you make me feel." Something more accurate describing my state of lust. Let's be clear, lust is a great thing, and it becomes greater and amplified when you mix it with love. However, when love and lust are confused at an early age, it creates emotional trauma. The type of trauma that makes one say:

- I will never love anyone again.
- I can't trust anyone.
- All men and women are the same.
- I will build walls to protect my mind and heart.
- Never again.

All of the above manifested as I listened to love songs and turned them off fast because now the lyrics hurt rather than comfort me to spark that tingle within. I waited by the phone, clinging to the hope she'll contact me. These were the Nokia phone days, and a call or real SMS message was the communication method—no social media channels or blocking drama back then. So what happens is I eventually get over the relationship and move on, in my case, putting on some weight after an unhealthy few weeks of playing the victim. However, I brought emotional baggage with me along with weight gain. I operated within the walls of safety, never being fully emotionally available to my next partner.

Our past relationships make us judge every man or woman we will meet in the foreseeable future. Learning to love yourself means forgiveness of your younger version. I hardly knew what love and lust were as a teenager, so I had to forgive my younger self as he did the best he could with the information he had. I had to remind myself I was loveable and worthy of love, and my partner or partners will come my way.

Most importantly, I had to convince myself I was complete. We do not need someone else to complete us. That is our job as we learn to grow, love ourselves, and become confident. Once you start believing in yourself again, knowing you are loveable and solidifying your inner confidence, it will boost your ability to find healthy relationships. It will make you attractive and ready to find love. Finding someone to love again is easier when you set better guidelines to operate in instead of going in blind without boundaries, communication, and a plan. There are close to eight billion people on the planet. So you never lose the love of your life since you have yet to find them.

Lesson 3:
Learn to Love Again with
Better Communication and Boundaries

After experiencing a breakup, I hesitated about reopening to love and dating again. It's normal to feel like you don't want to put yourself in a vulnerable position again, or fear that you might end up in another heartbreak.

However, it's important to remember that opening up to love and dating again can be a healthy and rewarding experience.

A critical step towards opening up to love and dating again is taking the time to heal from your previous relationship. I rushed into relationships because, once again, it was arising from a place of lust, ego, and the limiting belief that I needed validation by being with someone.

Give yourself the space and time to process your emotions and reflect on what you've learned from your past relationship. Focus on yourself, practice self-care, and engage in activities that bring you joy and fulfillment. Being single was a beautiful experience as I learnt to find my authentic self, not the one that needed to be with someone to prove a point.

Once I felt ready to start dating again, it was essential to approach the experience with an open mind and heart. Keep in mind that each relationship is unique and can offer something different. Avoid comparing your new partner to your ex; instead, focus on getting to know them deeply. Delete the ex from dating conversations. If asked on a date, ensure you speak honestly; if you mess up, it's okay. That red flag means you are still healing, and that level of honesty is a reasonable starting ground for something new.

Communication is vital in any relationship, so being open and honest about your feelings and expectations from the beginning is essential. This approach can help prevent misunderstandings and ensure that both parties are on the same page.

Setting healthy boundaries for yourself and your new relationship is also essential. Take things at a pace that feels comfortable for you, and don't feel pressured to rush into anything that doesn't feel right. Remember that saying no is okay if something doesn't align with your values or boundaries.

Opening up to love and dating again after a breakup can be a beautiful and transformative experience. It may take time and effort, but you can find a fulfilling and healthy relationship by being patient and kind to yourself. This kindness and compassion increase when you surround yourself with amazing people.

Lesson 4:
Surround Yourself with Amazing Friends

Many of my successful, healthier relationships have emerged from friendships. What is the secret? It's getting to know each other. Rushing into intimacy without knowing each other means there is room for incompatibility and mismatch. Rushing into intimacy and then returning to friendship can be awkward for some. However, I have learnt patience is a great practice to have. You get to know the other person and start feeling an energetic and emotional connection.

Resisting the urge of lust can be very rewarding, as it allows you to have a wider group of friends. Also, it enables you to receive social support and emotional engagement to have a healthier life. Even when in a romantic relationship, always have your friends with you. Having a quality group of people around you allows you to have balance and fun. It is not your lover's job to handle all your emotions and situations.

Having the label of friendship with your potential person of interest allows you space to breathe and be yourself. Let's face it, whenever I'm on a date, that engagement comes with expectations and behavioral modification to look desirable—too much pressure. I was instead hanging with friends, whether in a group or one to one. There was no pressure.

We chill, talk, connect, and get to understand each other. I could feel that energetic and emotional connection in such interactions. You feel safe and happy around them. If there is that attraction and lust, you both will feel the sexual energy, and it's okay to talk about it. Let them know you enjoy being around them, and if they feel the same, "more than a friend" vibe, experiment with the possibilities, because you don't want to run the risk of waking up in ten years saying what if? I have experienced that if the friendship is strong and the relationship doesn't work out, then you don't lose a friend. It only makes you stronger.

The friend zone is the modern-day quicksand in relationships. This term is a relational concept, portraying a situation in which one person in a mutual friendship desires to enter into a romantic or sexual relationship with the other person who does not. I recently had a random conversation with two New Yorkers in Dubai while on vacation. I heard one say,

"Once you are in the friend zone, there is no coming back." I rarely break into laughter at a stranger's comment, but I had to invite myself into their conversation to discuss the "why" in her statement.

You could break the Friendzone barrier by giving voice to your feelings.

Communication and honesty are potent tools. Silence and lack of expression can get you friend-zoned in relationships. In life, I had hesitated to speak when words needed to be said. However, I have learnt the power of words to shape my life and those in it. Sentences like:

- "I like you more than a friend, but not ready to go there as I'm healing from my previous relationship. I would love to get to know you better and be part of your life, and we can discuss this in-depth as we learn and grow together as friends for now."
- "I enjoy being around you, and you inspire me to be better. I can't quite describe my feelings, but let us continue this and have more awesome experiences."
- "I love and appreciate you as a person and friend, and I am open to the possibilities of loving you so much more, but in the words of John Legend, I'm taking it slow. However, I just wanted to let you know."

There is clarity when you express your intentions with words from a place of love. With effective communication, growth and seeds of trust are planted. Speaking about how you feel allows for better interaction than giving the person a dozen red roses without a note. Especially in the friendship phase, that flower move will scare the other person. I've been there and made that move, and I can share here that it's not a wise idea. Communication in any relationship is the key to peace of mind and the growth of that relationship.

When you verbalize your intention and feelings, not coming from a place of desperation but rather from a place of love, this approach strengthens the impact of the conversation on both parties. You will earn respect for speaking your truth and taking the time to listen to theirs. In the worst-case scenario, you might get a restraining order. I haven't experienced that, but just putting it out there.

Back to the wholesome topic of communication, sometimes the truth of where the other person is in life might not match your desired outcome, and it is better to have that known than guessing what the other person is feeling. Life is too short to guess what the other person is feeling, thinking, and experiencing. We have the gift of communication, so use it to optimize your relationships. When things don't go as desired, remember what I said earlier: There are soon to be eight billion people in the world, so the love of your life is still out there. And you still have friends in the process of finding the one.

Final Words

It's impossible to completely prevent heartbreak, as it's a natural aspect of life's journey. It's how we deal with it, heal from it, and continue to show up ready to love. In this chapter, I offered four lessons I wish I'd known when I was younger, as they could have saved me time, energy, and resources while sparing me heartbreak.

Ram Dass famously advised us to *"Speak the truth and love everybody."* I've realized that the truth holds immense power, as it frees us from the drama and emotional strain that come with avoiding it. To uncover the truth, we must detach from our ego, a process that becomes easier with practice. Though speaking the truth may sometimes result in the loss of a relationship, it's crucial to remember that if someone cannot accept the real you, then they were not meant to be in your life.

With this in mind, forgiveness and love should always be our guiding principles. We must forgive and persist forward to find our one in eight billion.

There is no space for hate in our hearts, only love. I don't want to make it sound like a cheesy bumper sticker, but coming from a place of love allows us to expand. That expansion makes us attractive to others, whether they be friends or lovers. Making the shift from platonic to romantic is possible and a recommended path.

Friendship and social life are highly valued, especially after the lockdown. I continue to come from a place of love and surround myself with similar amazing people. This approach leads to many bromantic moments, finding a new sister from a different mister, and occasionally you meet someone with romantic sparks. The latter romance scenario will excite some single people and might scare some already in a relationship. In either situation, you don't have to act on it right away, be comfortable being friends to get to know each other, and you will both know what to do when the time feels right.

That felt like the preview tease for the next book. And it is! See below for information about my book. For now, remember the four lessons:

1. Know the difference between love and lust.
2. Learn to love yourself first.
3. Learn to love again with better communication and boundaries.
4. Surround yourself with amazing friends.

Utilizing these lessons judiciously and applying common sense can completely revolutionize your love life and relationships. Anything is achievable when you have faith in yourself, practice self-love and self-forgiveness, surround yourself with amazing people, and remain open to possibilities.

Tell the truth and love everybody.
-Ram Dass

About the Author

Faraaz Ali focuses on high performance, productivity, and positivity in high-pressure situations to create possibility and prosperity for his clients.

Faraaz has explored over seventy-five countries while building his educational content. Thirty-two of these countries were with his daughter before she turned three. So creating new ways to handle parenting, leadership, remote offices, and managing new environments & cultures while maintaining high operational efficiency is something he lives by and teaches.

Starting his career in IT and television, he has evolved into a lifestyle and culture strategist for entrepreneurial parents to help shape the new world. His methodology builds on spirituality and zen philosophies. He focuses on creating a world full of empathy, compassion, clarity, and connectivity to elevate humanity. One mind at a time.

Author Contact Information

Website: www.faraazali.com
Instagram: www.instagram.com/faraaz4real

The Path is Winding

by Kerry Fisher

You need to keep your emotions in balance,
treading that fine line between commitment to your goals
and disappointment when they do not come to fruition,
whilst still being optimistic and positive about the future.

~Tom Laurie

A h...the struggle is real, folks. The journey toward becoming the best version of yourself isn't a path for the faint-hearted. It's a journey marked by towering peaks and deep valleys, a journey that can bring you to your knees. Let me transport you back to a moment of soul-shaking darkness that I experienced years ago.

At that time, my career aspiration was crystal clear: to become an author and a speaker. I was diligently pursuing this goal, pouring my efforts into shaping the career of my dreams. I was unwavering in my focus, making significant strides toward realizing my loftiest career ambitions. Then, a pivotal moment arrived. I reached out to Mindvalley, a company I deeply admired, hoping to become a meditation teacher and ultimately an author on their platform. The prospect seemed promising, and I engaged in conversations with the responsible individual. She expressed interest in my work, but weeks later, the crushing blow came – they decided not to move forward. It felt like a devastating defeat.

I was within arm's reach of my aspirations, only to watch them slip through my fingers. The news hit me like a ton of bricks. Tears welled up, and I felt the impact viscerally, a gut punch that left me breathless, and not in a good way. You've likely experienced that sensation, right?

Devastation washed over me, but amid the turmoil, the words of my favorite author, Paulo Coelho, resonated with me. In the prologue of the 2002 version of "The Alchemist," Coelho eloquently narrates the hero's journey. Curiously, despite having read the book countless times, I had only recently encountered this particular prologue. It arrived at the perfect moment, revealing the obstacles that block our path to discovering our treasure, our dream life, our true selves.

Childhood to adulthood, we're told repeatedly that our dreams are impossible, that we're bound to fail. Overcoming this initial barrier, we encounter the obstacle of love – the fear that pursuing our dreams might distance us from those we care for. Triumphing over this, the next challenge is the fear of failure, a hurdle familiar to us all.

When my dream job slipped from my grasp, I grappled not only with fear of failure, but with actual failure as my cherished dream slipped away. The sting was sharp, leaving me shattered. You see, when you pour your heart into pursuing your deepest desires and fall short, recovering isn't easy.

Doubt creeps in – perhaps you're inadequate, not up to the task. That's precisely how I felt: utterly defeated.

As is my custom during stressful times, I brewed a cup of tea, grabbed a good book, and sought solace in a warm bath. Tears may or may not have accompanied the experience. In the bath's embrace, I allowed pain, self-doubt, and disappointment to course through me. And then, as I emerged from the bath, I watched the water drain, imagining my troubles flowing away with it. A semblance of relief crept in, a weight lifted.

In that moment, I made a decision. I resolved to pick myself up, to press onward toward my goal. Step by step, I committed to honing my skills, refining my message, and doing whatever it took to actualize my dream. I knew I would reach that destination someday, even if that day wasn't today.

And that, my friends, embodies the essence of the hero's journey. It's an expedition marked by ascents and descents. The highs are euphoric, the lows, excruciating. Yet, that's how growth happens, isn't it? It's the reason we refer to challenges as "growing pains." The near-attainment of my Mindvalley dream proved to be a pivotal moment. Normally, I might have abandoned that particular dream, concluding it wasn't meant for me. But this time, armed with tools gathered over years, I recommitted to my aspirations. Mindvalley was still part of my vision, and I wouldn't let a single rejection deter my momentum. I refused to be thwarted that day.

I shifted my focus to what it would take to become a Mindvalley author. I realized I didn't need to wait for Mindvalley's affirmation. Instead, I needed to craft a body of work that would draw Mindvalley to me. A body of work that would make them want me in their cadre of authors. Armed with this realization, I crafted a to-do list and set it into motion.

I knew I had to complete the book I'd been putting off – *"The Snooze Button Sessions,"* a manuscript I'd started years earlier. With a library of content amassed over a decade of teaching mindfulness, yoga, peak performance, and mindset, I found I had an abundance of material at my fingertips. Reading through the half-finished manuscript, I recognized its quality and decided to finish it. Completing that book ignited a surge of creativity within me. Today, I immerse myself in the world of writing, crafting daily for hours on end. Astonishingly, one of my greatest disappointments became the catalyst for my success.

> *Nothing in life occurs to you; it occurs for you.*
> *Every letdown, every misstep,*
> *even every slammed door contributes to shaping who you are.*
> ~Joel Ostten

So, when life derails your plans, what's your recourse? Who will you turn to? I'd love to jest "Ghostbusters," but in reality, a toolkit of strategies might be your best bet. Here's a glimpse of the tools that aided me in times of discouragement – and let's be honest, it wasn't just discouragement; it was heartache, devastation. Yet, these tools countered the pain, propelling me forward. They proved so effective that I've outlined a simple framework you can follow should you ever find yourself in the same boat.

1. Support: I reached out to two individuals: my husband and a wise friend I'd encountered through Mindvalley. Over the past year, I've cultivated a circle of like-minded friends from the platform. While I used to confide in my mother during tough times, it typically didn't yield positive results. Her inability to come to terms with my transition from attorney to a different path – I'm 56 now, you see – cast a shadow on our conversations. Whenever we discussed my career, she'd quip, "Sorry your little job isn't going well." Not exactly uplifting, I must say. The lesson: discern who to reach out to and, perhaps even more crucially, who not to reach out to.

2. Inspiration: I relistened to "Awaken the Species" to be reminded of my greater mission: helping people become the individuals they dream of being, guiding them towards their true purpose so they can live the epic life of their dreams. I listened to the course while in the bath, with candles and incense burning. Ambiance matters. Lesson: Use your tools.

3. Release: I went straight to meditation, eliminating the limiting beliefs that arose from the rejection. After I got out of the bath, I made a sign saying, "I AM ENOUGH." Okay, I made two signs. Lesson: Use your tools. P.S. Crying works well here too, lol.

4. Take Action: After I completed all the above, I took massive action towards my goals – continually enhancing my skills and transforming, perhaps even merging into the person I need to become for my goals to come true. I got a ton of work done on my course and book. Lesson: Action is always the answer. Massive action is even better.

5. Relax: Then, I watched a movie with my son on Netflix while eating nachos, even though dairy and I don't get along. (Hey, I'm human.) Most important during the relaxation phase is to remember to go easy on yourself. You don't have to be perfect. And remember to lean on those who love you. Friends and family are like a warm blanket, keeping you warm when you need it.

> *Between stimulus and response, there is a space.*
> *In that space is our power to choose our response.*
> *In our response lies our growth and our freedom.*
> -Victor Frankl

So, next time something doesn't go your way, remember that space and remember that you have a choice. You can throw yourself down on your knees and cry out to the universe, "WHY?" in a sobbing kind of way (swear, I've never done that, lol), OR you can choose to remember your tools and, most importantly, use them. Taking action is the best response to any setback. Remember, action is always the antidote to any negative emotion. Take action, deal with what you need to, and then pick yourself back up and get after it! I'll be rooting for you, and I'll be rooting for me too. I'm rooting for all of us.

XO Kerry

Lesson: Whenever life knocks you down, take some time to recalibrate, and then get back out there and take action – massive action – towards your goals.

> *You are chosen, and your job is to just take the order and make it happen.*
> -Vishen Lakhiani

Postscript

Two years after the experience I related above, I found myself in Tallinn, Estonia for an amazing Mindvalley meetup. About ninety people from around the world had come to meet with Vishen and the Mindvalley team for a Christmas celebration weekend. It was the first time people had gathered since the beginning of the coronavirus pandemic. We ate, drank, and danced all night long.

One of the nights was dubbed the White and Gold Party. We all donned our white and gold glittery evening wear and went off to have fun. We danced and danced and danced.

Then, the founder of the company, Vishen Lakhiani, called all of us together and began to give a speech about one of the people he wanted to thank. He said he had created the Mindvalley Heroes Award, and this person was going to be the first person to receive it. Then he called my name and gave ME the award. I was struck speechless, which never happens.

Vishen handed me the award and then asked all the men to gather around me for an epic picture. There I was, in a glittery gold princess dress, surrounded by men in their finest. It was a moment I shall cherish – my golden moment in the sun.

Even more amazing, a mere six months after that, I found myself on the Mindvalley Stage giving a speech about my first book. And then, not even a year later, during an incredible three weeks, I was given the opportunity to be the host on the Mindvalley stage, announcing the speakers.

As I stood on the Mindvalley Stage, I had such an intense moment of gratitude when I realized in a flash that I had become an author and was learning to become a speaker. My dreams were coming true! And it reminded me once again that when we keep our eyes on the destination and keep moving towards it despite any obstacles, magic and mystery abound!

About the Author

Kerry is an author, a speaker, and a wellness educator. She is a licensed attorney who left her law career to pursue an extraordinary life.

Her mission is to help others find a more balanced and fulfilled life. She believes in action and she teaches Simple Tips for Extraordinary Living using stress reduction techniques and work-life balance to help people supercharge their lives. She coaches corporate clients and elite athletes in mindset and peak performance techniques and creates tailored programs for private clients who are seeking mastery in all areas of their lives.

After many years of teaching and coaching, Kerry is focused on writing, creating courses and speaking on the topics she is so passionate about. She is on a mission to inspire and encourage people to become the person they dream of being and to create the life they imagine.

Author Contact Information

Website: kerryfishercoaching.com
Instagram: @kerryfisher
Email: iamkerryfisher@gmail.com
LinkedIn: www.linkedin.com/in/kerry-fisher-

Nothing in the world can take the place of persistence.
Talent will not; nothing is more common than
unsuccessful men with talent. Genius will not;
unrewarded genius is almost a proverb.
Education will not; the world is full of educated derelicts.
Persistence and determination alone are omnipotent.

~Calvin Coolidge

What Does Being a Hero Mean to You?

by Ivan Garcia

There is no happiness without freedom;
and there is no freedom without courage.

~Pericles

A simple question, dear reader, that can make us reflect about ourselves and the qualities that define us best. Have you ever thought deeply about what makes you, you? Beyond the fields of science, beyond chemistry or matter. We all have bodies made of the same elements, bound together by a mysterious force we have yet to understand. A never-ending cluster of stardust in a perpetual transformation cycle across the Cosmos.

I once heard a famous philosopher say that, if you ask someone to describe themself, it would be something like: "I am Ivan Garcia. I am a civil engineer, and I live in Lisbon, Portugal. I am a calm, creative, and joyful person, and I also like to travel." Surprisingly, that is what this person is *not*.

You might be asking yourself, "What? This seems like a simple and normal way to describe oneself. Of course we would say where we lived, what our job was, our attributes. That is what we are, is it not? As far as the philosopher was concerned, it was not.

Apparently, this idea of labeling our own self with predetermined ideas might be the easiest and most common way to determine who we are, however, this can also limit the way we see and feel about ourselves, significantly. Saying that I am a civil engineer will give me a sense of identity attached to this profession. This can make me feel comfortable whenever I am thinking about or doing anything related to it. But what if I don't relate myself to little or anything related to it? This can create an identity conflict. If you could see 20 different tonalities of green, would you use the word "green" for all of them? If so, maybe your perception would adapt to that thought, and you would actually see just one type of green.

At the end of the day, there is nothing wrong with building our identity around labels – as long as it works for us, rather than against us. Do we have to *be* a Hero, in order to do something heroic? Do we have to *be* a Hero, in order to feel like one? And how do we know if we are being the Hero of our own story, a mere spectator or worse – our own Nemesis? That, my friends, is the question I have asked myself my entire life.

Let me tell you the story of a young boy named Ari, who grew up in a labeling culture. Let me tell you how limited he was by it, how he became conscious of this, and how he went on his own incredible Hero's Journey, taking him into extraordinary adventures throughout the world. Adventures like solo backpacking through majestic mountains, scorching deserts, lush jungles, endless megacities, and even mysterious ruins of ancient human civilizations. From the very own valleys of the mind, eroded by storms of despair and fear, to the highest peaks of victory, baked by rays of fortune and bliss. This is a story of the transformation of the soul, and how we are meant to live our own Heroic Odyssey and inspire everyone in our path.

The pain of yesterday is the strength of the Warrior of the Light.
~Paulo Coelho

Humble Beginnings

Aristides was born in the 90's – a decade marked by cartoons, comic books, boy bands, three dimensional video games, indestructible cell phones, and oversized clothes. He was a curious boy in a stimulating world. His childhood was affected by a modern and globalized world, where "far away" was now a relative concept, due to the advent of a thriving young Internet. Although technology was abundant around him during his first decade of life, he enjoyed the simplicity of pencil and paper, playing with other kids, reading his favorite comic books, watching cartoons, spending time with his family, and dreaming of imaginary worlds. Little Ari had a fertile imagination and loved to put into paper the things he would vividly imagine in his mind. His favorite drawing subjects were dragons and other fantastic creatures. He grew up surrounded by animals, and it was easy for him to befriend and tame the most spectacular creatures in the worlds he created.

Ari's artistic and creative side came from his own mother. She was very talented with pencil and paper, and encouraged little Ari to allow himself to express and communicate through Art. Moreover, she had the most beautiful calligraphy he had ever seen in his life. She was always very loving and quite caring to him, nurturing his little heart with love and allowing him to dream big dreams. She was born in Angola, a Portuguese colony at the time.

Ari loved spending time with his father. His dad educated him on the importance of valuing and respecting nature and all beings. He would often take Ari out for outdoor activities and adventures. He taught little Ari about nature, but also about the importance of being healthy by keeping active and eating his fruits and vegetables. Ari's father was probably one of the biggest influences on Ari, imparting a sense of wonder and curiosity, as well as teaching Ari that it was good to question the rules of society.

Ari's father was a great communicator. He had proven himself several times as a top salesman and used that skill to "sell" his own ideas and views of the world to Ari. He was also a photography and technology enthusiast, with love for music, especially rock bands. He was born in Mozambique, also a Portuguese colony at the time.

Both his mother and his father passed on to Ari a set of values and skills that would shape his own life and made him the person he is today. Together, they showed him what a strong bond was like, and how a powerful union of two beings could create life itself. His parents' relationship was a great example of Unity and Love, and he was fortunate to learn from them. But they were not perfect. They would have their occasional arguments and disagreements, and also had a list of negative and toxic behaviors that would later be responsible for little Ari having to grow up away from their presence.

> *Children begin by loving their parents;*
> *as they grow older, they judge them;*
> *sometimes, they forgive them.*
> ~Oscar Wilde

Growing Up with the Elderly

Although Ari's parents always loved him, they had a hard time raising him, and Ari ended up being raised by his grandparents. This was painful to Ari, but it was a decision he would understand a bit later in his teenage years. Ari never rebelled against this, since he loved to be with his grandparents, and they were crucial in educating Ari with an important set of skills and values that would shape him for life.

Ari's grandfather was a hardworking man, who grew up on the streets of Lisbon and later moved to Angola, still young with his parents, as a result of the Portuguese emigration to this ex-colony. In Angola, he worked in the industry and transportation sectors, fought in the Colonial Wars, and worked in the diamond industry for many years. Ari's grandfather was a master storyteller, and he would regale Ari with tales of the war and other adventures during his time in Angola. He used to tell those stories at lunch time when the family was present, and would always add new little details every time he would tell the same story. Ari's sense of adventure and exploration might very well have come from his own grandfather and his tales of epic adventures.

Ari's greatest idol was his grandmother. The matriarch of the family was easily his biggest inspiration and role model. A compassionate and caring woman, loved by all, always ready to serve and provide for everyone around her. If there was a single person in his life who would show him the meaning of Unconditional Love, it was her. Mother of three, including Ari's mother, she was a super mother, who lived to serve her family the best way she could, while her husband was away working. Compassion, servitude to others, patience, and Unconditional Love were passed on to young Ari by this exemplar human being.

Many years before Ari was born, his grandparents and his still young parents lived a dramatic experience, while in Africa. Due to a military revolution in Portugal, in 1974, known as "April's Revolution", a treaty was signed to declare independence to the Portuguese colonies. This would mean that Angola and Mozambique would declare independence and assume their sovereignty. According to the reports and personal experience of Ari's grandparents, the radical and extreme way the Portuguese colonists had to leave those countries was described as nothing short of horrible and dramatic.

In a matter of hours after the independence was declared, his grandparents had to rush and fly their families out of the country, with the emerging menace of the militia and local armed forces invading their homes and aggressively forcing them out, or worse – killing them all.

Can you imagine this situation, dear reader? You have made your life in your place of choice, and provided your family with enough comfort and conditions for having a peaceful life, with the fruits of your hard work in life. You have your normal routine, your loving pets, your friends, and your business up and running. You live a fulfilling life, only to find yourself being forced to leave with your family with nothing but your clothes and leave everything else behind you in a matter of hours, or be killed alongside your family in a war that you never asked for.

How would you feel? Afraid? Angry? Anxious? Desperate? Confused? Ari's grandparents felt all of that and more. It was a traumatic time for the family.

More than a decade after this episode, Ari was born and had the blessing of living in a war-free environment. He spent most of his life with his grandparents and learned many valuable lessons from them. They did their best to make sure he was happy and healthy, providing him with the most important things in life.

Neale Donald Walsch, in his famous Conversations with God, Volume III, wrote that children should primarily be educated not by their parents or teachers, but by their grandparents. His writings suggested that the younger generations would benefit the most from learning directly from the most experienced generations, hence the importance of spending time with the elderly. Parents, especially young parents, are still in their own process of growing up, making mistakes and learning from those mistakes. They have little to teach to their offspring and most times they don't even have the time to teach anything, whatsoever. Sadly, they outsource their children's education to the system, which can be ruthless over the years. The elderly, on the other hand, have the time, will, knowledge and wisdom of a lifetime in their hands, ready to be passionately shared. Just stop and think about it for a second.

Let us imagine a scenario where you, dear reader, are about to enter the Game of Life, and have very little experience of it. You just posted a new ad, looking for a teacher to help you go through and understand Life. In the first hour you receive two contacts:

Candidate A – Adal, 28 years old

Hi, Ivan! My name is Adal and I saw your post for a Life Teacher. I have 28 years of experience in this field. Currently I am doing my best to build a good career, keeping myself healthy, working on my financial independence, and working on my relationship with my partner. We plan to buy a house, have children, and travel the world. My dream is to have my own business and make a good name for myself. At the moment my time is limited, but I am willing to teach you all I know for you to be successful in Life.

Candidate B – Albert, 86 years old

Dear Ivan,

My name is Albert, an 86 year old veteran in the game of Life. I've lived many experiences and have many stories to share with you. I've been healthy and unhealthy, wealthy and poor, single and married, divorced and married again. I've worked for others, for myself and for Humanity. I've lived alone and I've lived in good company. I've lived in peace and I've lived in a war place. I've been the Hero and I've been the Villain. My greatest learnings in life came from my biggest mistakes and my greatest achievements came from humility, perseverance and faith. I've built many meaningful relationships with people around me and I still nurture them. My partner and my family are at the top of the most important things in my life.

My time on this journey is not over yet, and I will be around here for some more time. I have all the time to be with you and share my own experiences and lessons in this Life.

Like I mentioned in the beginning, you are about to enter the Game of Life and you are looking for a mentor. Someone who already knows something about the game. Someone who, despite any belief or cultural background, gender or race, can introduce you to the fundamentals of such a mysterious and complex game. Who would you pick? The young and enthusiastic Adal, with his brief experience and time limited schedule, or the old and experienced Albert, with plenty of time and wisdom to share with you?

If you are like me and wanted to get the edge in the game right from the beginning of this adventure of Life, Albert would be the obvious choice.

What would you ask him first? What knowledge would you like this wise human being to share with you right away? If I could, my first question would be: "What does being a Hero mean to you?"

This sidenote, dear reader, is just to demonstrate that sometimes, in our lives, the greatest teachers and coaches are already next to us, and we only understand that later in Life. They can be in our family, in our friends' circle, in a club, a sports team, a work group, or we can even learn a valuable lesson from a different species than ours.

And what about little Ari, you must be thinking. He was fortunate enough to spend most of his life learning from the elderly, his grandparents. They were the very first real life Heroes he got to witness and admire. They had no special costumes, no special nicknames, no superhuman powers, no fancy vehicles, nor no castle on the hills to live and rule. They were simply human and vulnerable. They taught him about the game of life. They were his heroes.

Who are the Heroes of your own life? What lessons have they taught you? How have they influenced you and the people around them?

John C. Maxwell frequently said that "leaders create other leaders". If we replace "leaders" with "heroes", the idea sticks. Heroes are people that inspire us. Not just for what they do or their life story, but essentially for who they are. Their actions motivate us, their mission inspires us, and their presence empowers us. It's in their essence, and we feel it.

Years have passed and Ari understands now what it means to be a Hero. He has written this short story for you, dear reader. The young boy who grew up in a label culture is me. I am Ari, and I am sharing this story so that I can share with you what it means to be a hero:

> *Being a Hero means to lead by example, being*
> *the best version of yourself you can be,*
> *influencing others to be their best, showing compassion*
> *and unconditional love for those around you and*
> *not being afraid to be vulnerable.*
> -Ivan Garcia

As a good friend of mine, Nolan Pillay, says: "Are you going through pain, or are you growing through pain?" Failing is inevitable. Giving up is a choice.

> *When you improve, everything else around you improves.*
> -Ken Wilber

The Hero Within

Life is our greatest teacher, and we are eternal students. As Bob Proctor said once: "Your attitude towards Life determines Life's attitude towards you." Life is our greatest teacher, and it is always sending lessons our way. We will face these lessons, inevitably. Some will be pleasant and fun. Others will be cruel and painful. Some will make our hearts glow and shine. Others will hurt and leave deep scars. So it is in this Rollercoaster of Life.

Every Hero had to go through all sorts of trials and challenges in order to magnify who they become. The brightest stars started with the smallest spark, and that never prevented them from becoming what they were meant to be.

When life is kind and throws pleasant lessons at you, rejoice and enjoy. Be present and feel each moment as a gift of Life to you. When Life is harsh and puts you down, take a break, get up, breathe, and move on. Life is not meant to be easy, nor difficult, nor perfect nor complicated. Life is meant to be lived. We are given a huge canvas to paint whatever way we want. We are the ultimate artists and creators of this magnificent masterpiece that is Life. There is no right or wrong way to paint it. There is only our way. Let us be free to express our own creativity, and paint the most magnificent artwork we can ever create, adding it to this Universal Gallery and making everything better in the process.

You, like me and many others, are meant to join this Hero's call, for we are all on our own Hero's journey. We are beings of light and shadow with more to offer to this world than we ever imagined.

Allow yourself to use your own unique gifts and talents to make this a better world to live in, serving our species and influencing others around us to do the same. It is much more than just what you can do. It is who you can be. Who you are meant to be.

You are the Hero of your own story. A story of many tales, events, defeats, victories, losses, and achievements. If you aim for greatness and victory, failure will meet you eventually. Failure is inevitable. Giving up is a choice. Choose how you want to continue creating your own story. A story in which you are the creator. The world needs and calls for you. You do not need any superpowers. You just have to believe in yourself and Be You.

Now go, dear Hero. It's time for you to shine your light bright and inspire everyone around you, in your epic journey to become the best you can be.

Shine and Inspire.
~Ivan Garcia

About the Author

Ivan was born in Lisbon, Portugal, in 1990. He studied science and graduated in Civil Engineering. Although he worked as an engineer during his life, his true calling and passion has always been teaching English and helping others improve their Communication skills in a natural and engaging way. He believes in a world where Education is seen as sacred, making Humanity better in every way possible, being accessible to everyone. Thus, one of his missions in life is to contribute to the evolution of Education and optimize Human Communication to suit the rapid-growing flow of information and connectedness in the world.

Awarded with Competent Communicator and Competent Leader distinctions by Toastmasters International, he has been using the power of effective communication to optimize his service to others, empowering people with the tools for them to better express themselves.

For over a decade he has worked with hundreds of people to change their own paradigms about how they learn and communicate, and helped them improve their lives and the lives of those around them.

Author Contact Information

LinkedIn: https://www.linkedin.com/in/ifgarcia/
Instagram: https://www.instagram.com/ivan.garcla

The Power of POEMS

by Dani Glaeser

In the darkest moment of our lives, we realized we had a choice.
We could choose how we responded.
We chose to make the most of our situation, to seek out the gifts,
open to opportunity, and make a difference in the lives we touched.

~Dani Glaeser

My beloved was getting worse. He'd lost the nerve function in his legs from the knees down. His energy was fading fast, and now he was losing the nerves in his hands. We managed to get him into Johns Hopkins for further evaluation, since he was wait-listed for the Mayo Clinic in Minnesota. And it was there they discovered he had a cancerous lesion on his hip bone, and he was diagnosed with POEMS syndrome.

I still remember how my heart sank when I read about what having POEMS syndrome was, what could happen, and the time lines attached. I went to him, held onto him as we processed the possibilities. I remember the hard conversations we had to have about what to do if he didn't make it through.

In that moment, when the world around us seemed as though it turned upside down, when life as we knew it felt as though it were ending, we made the choice to make the most of the situation. We would not be victims. We would find the gifts, be open to opportunities, we would shift priorities, we would unite and make our way through it – wherever our journey might lead. If we could use what happened to us, to help or inspire even one other person in this world, then, it would be worth it.

In July of 2018, my world as I knew it came to a screeching halt. I was faced with the possible death of my husband to a rare syndrome called POEMS, which was ironically the same name for how I processed my stress. Now, the word POEMS took on a whole new meaning in my life.

When I was younger and dealing with pain, I would convert it into poetry. My poems contained tears, pain, all the emotions that I wanted to work through transcribed into words on a page. When I wanted to move through something, I used poetry. But this type of POEMS offered me no solace, no way to process. I had to find my own way.

The fear welled up as I read what POEMS entailed, when I saw there was a time limit to it, when I read about it. I told my kids, whatever you do – do not look it up. I didn't want to add to their fear and their building anxiety over what was happening with their father. I grieved, I screamed, I got angry. I felt all the feelings. And then I went to him, placed my forehead upon his, and we held one another.

This was not our vision for our future. This was not what we wanted to deal with, and yet, we had to deal with it, one way or another.

We knew that despite his diagnosis, we had the power of choice. We got to choose how we wanted to deal with the situation and how we wanted to live our lives. We understood at that moment that we were the ones who got to choose how we reacted. We were the ones that got to choose how to spend whatever time we had together. As we made this commitment to each other, I could feel something rise up from the depths within me. Whatever happened, we would get through it. Whatever happened, we would deal with it. Whatever happened, we would move forward.

We chose to seek out the gifts and be open to opportunities. We chose to grow, and transform through this situation. We were already grieving the loss of what was, our vision was halted. We had to learn to live in the moment. It was time to be fully present, to make the most of the time we had together.

Rising up we chose
to commit to each other
We would get through this.
~Dani Glaeser

We didn't know what would happen in five years, but we still held fast to our vision. Our mantra became "Step by step, we move forward" and we said this even when he became wheelchair bound. In December of 2017, when he had lost the nerves from his knees down, and we didn't yet know it was POEMS, we discovered a program called Lifebook through Mindvalley. It intrigued us because the concept was that we should look at all areas of our life and decide how we wanted to show up in that area. We decided to do the program because we realized that we had never bothered to examine our beliefs, our values, our vision, our whys, or create strategies on our own to get what we wanted. So we decided to do that now, at this critical juncture in our lives, at a point when we weren't sure of the future.

We started the program, and we went deep. Examining our lives and deciding what we wanted gave us something we could control amidst the space of the unknown. It gave us the power to dream, hope, and design the life we wanted. It would become our lifeline, a raft in the sea of the unknown, during the really hard times. Lifebook gave us a vessel to contain our dreams, and to ponder how to make these dreams our reality. It gave us a purpose, something to hold onto when life shifted and uncertainty reigned.

I had been a part of Mindvalley, which is a personal growth educational company, for quite a while. I was drawn into its courses when I injured my back in 2012. I discovered Silva meditations through Mindvalley – and they really helped to make a difference in the pain and my healing. I had continued to listen to the Silva meditations and a lot of the other content on Mindvalley and I really enjoyed it. I didn't realize it at the time, however, as I listened to these mediations and learned about different modalities of health and wellness, my mindset was shifting. I was getting stronger, clearer and more focused. Looking back, it almost seems as though I was preparing for what was to come on some level.

I had the opportunity to meet the creators of Lifebook and Mindvalley. It was an incredible experience. I remember the first time I met Vishen, the founder of Mindvalley. I didn't even introduce myself, I just asked if I could hug him, and then we hugged. I was beyond grateful, and just so excited to finally express my gratitude in person. The programs he was bringing forth into the world via the Mindvalley Platform, helped me in my times of darkness. I knew that I was only one of many. His Be Extraordinary quest and his 6 Phase Meditation were super powerful for me, and were both a part of me creating a new mindset and practicing forgiveness for myself and others. (Little did I realize how important that would be.)

All of the things I had learned helped me during our darkest moments. As my beloved and I embraced the space of the unknown, we had to deal with the unexpected as well. I became a full time caregiver, and took on his roles and responsibilities in our family. He dealt with guilt over not being able to contribute. Our two children were facing major anxiety over the possible loss of their dad.

To add to this, we had two incidents with people in our lives whom we cared about that were incredibly painful. Looking back now, it is clear to me that they were dealing with their own pain, and were absorbed in their own stories. But when it happened, it was another jolt to my world. I was rocked to the core of my being, feeling hurt, angry, betrayed. It took me a while to grieve what was, and accept what happened.

This was a very rough time for us, and the complication of having people I loved seemingly turning on me was a lot for me to deal with. The first time it happened was right after we discovered that my beloved's neuropathy treatments were not improving his condition. His neurologist tried to refer us to the Mayo clinic. I was carrying the weight of this on my shoulders, trying to process it all. The Mayo Clinic? Seriously? This shocked us as we had thought we were headed in the right direction, only to discover that there was a sharp curve, taking us off the path we were on.

Right as this was going on, I had called to check in with someone I cared about, to see if they had gotten a card I'd sent. Next thing I know, the texts got weird, and when I questioned some things, it turned into them wanting to talk to me on the phone. I had no clue that the next hour would turn out the way it did. My beloved ended up sitting next to me as the others on the phone yelled at me, expressing their bitter anger, threw false accusations at me, and eventually told me they wanted distance.

It appeared that they wanted me to act a certain way and do things their way. I tend to ask a lot of questions, especially so I can better understand, and this only seemed to anger them. I also let people work things out between themselves. Taking sides in the past had gotten me into a lot of trouble, so I'd stopped getting involved. I'd changed my role as an enabler. If you've ever changed a role you played from childhood, it can be really hard for those who are used to your old patterns to accept your new role, especially if the old role benefited them. My friend had expectations of me, and when I didn't meet them, it was easier to put distance between us. I could respect that, and so I honored the request for distance, and what that really meant.

As a result of this emotional conversation with my friend, I ended up ill for a month. My upset affected my beloved, as he watched me process the pain of the distance, trying to understand why things happened the way they did, and grieve the loss of people I loved. I grieved the fact that we didn't have the relationship that I thought, and that they didn't know me as I thought they did. I grieved the realization that I had spent years putting them before my own family, going out of my way to keep connections, only to see that they didn't even recognize my contributions.

I faced my own expectations of them and our relationship. Ah yes, expectations. I had to let them go and move to acceptance on my own end. At the end of the month, we swore that we would not allow this to happen again. We would put ourselves and our family first. We knew that at this moment in time, my beloved's health was of utmost importance.

We stripped it down to the barest minimum. We got essential at this point. We set boundaries, and upheld them.

A few months later, when we got the diagnosis of POEMS, these people reached out to offer help, and I said no. I was still feeling really emotional, and hearing their voices caused me to feel nauseous. Here I was processing my own grief and discovery of what being diagnosed with POEMS meant, and then I was feeling the tension from the angry call. When the other wrote to me to say how sorry they were, instead of reconnecting and making excuses for them, as I would have in the past, I kept distance and set firm boundaries.

During my call with them, I realized a few things. They had no clue who I was as a person, and they had expectations of me that I wasn't meeting, and wasn't willing to meet because they were unhealthy. I also realized I no longer knew who these people were, and had set my own expectations. The entire experience awakened me on many levels. I chose to grow from it.

About seven months later, I would get to experience another situation, in which a person who I thought I knew and could depend on, turned out to be dealing with their own pain and frustration. I knew they had a pattern, that when things didn't go as they wanted or expectations weren't met, they created a toxic atmosphere with their behavior and words, especially when they were feeling insignificant. In the past, it was easier to deal with, and I did my best to diffuse the situation. This time, they chose to vent during a time when I was exhausted, processing my beloved being in the hospital as his condition worsened, and trying to make food for my kids for the next day.

I could've chosen to put a stop to it, then and there, but I knew that my kids and the rest of the family would have to deal with the fallout. My priority was keeping things as calm as possible for my husband's benefit. So, I chose to listen to their story, breathed through the anger when they lied to me, and realized I no longer wanted this energy or this person in my life. I had come to the point of no return. I was done.

When this person finally left, I felt so relieved and grateful. The energy in the entire environment shifted. What did I learn from this? I could have set boundaries and stopped them, I could have called them out on their lies, but I didn't. I made choices based on the greater good, and what was best for me at the moment. I chose to give myself grace – as I did the best I could with what I had.

There is a concept called Kensho and Satori moments. A Kensho moment is "growth from pain" while Satori moments are "when you grow from an insight or Aha moment". I was experiencing Satori moments within Kensho moments at this point.

The thing that saved me was meditation. I was doing the 6 Phase Meditation at this time and one part of the meditation focuses on forgiveness. I would do the forgiveness part of the 6 Phase Meditation each morning, and sometimes, a few times during the day. As I did the meditation, I realized that I needed to process my intense anger. It got to the point where I knew I needed help. Eventually, I found a trusted therapist who helped me to dive deep and really work through the anger. As I went through the therapy, I was able to grieve the loss since in both situations, I deeply cared for the people. Eventually, I was able to totally forgive them, and move beyond.

I can now look back at these moments with pure gratitude. These Kensho moments have become very powerful gifts. Yes, there was pain, but I was able to grow in ways I wouldn't have otherwise. As a result, I see people differently now, and I practice compassion.

I also discovered something else that was powerful. When people leave your life, it opens space for others to enter. And when you aren't spending energy worrying about upsetting others, thinking about what you could have done differently, or just being angry, you become lighter. My energy shifted. I no longer carried the worry of having to spend time with someone who left me feeling drained, and who's behavior created a heaviness in the environment.

Since 2018, there's been so much growth amidst the pain. I am very different now than I was when the diagnosis happened, and I love who I have become. In fact, I'm getting more daring with the life vision I created in Lifebook. We've had to update it a few times, because we keep achieving the goals we set out for ourselves, so we push ourselves to dream even bigger, to create grander visions for ourselves, our family, and our future.

Lifebook has allowed us to live smart in all areas of our lives. It has brought an awareness to how we live, and to what is best for ourselves, and our family. It kept us grounded in the space of the unknown, and gave us a vision to anchor into. When you are in the space of the unknown, or feeling lost, your vision is your guiding star. It's your hope, your reminder of where you are going. I continue to learn more about myself, and really hone in on what is best for me, what will pull me towards my life vision.

I perceive life differently since Mindvalley and, especially, the Lifebook course. I have gotten very involved in both companies, becoming an ambassador in each of those communities. It has been beautiful.

My focus has shifted. I no longer ask, "Why me?" but ask, "What can I learn? What is the gift? How can I grow?" I am open to opportunities that I wasn't before. Gratitude and compassion are my practices. I honor the Kensho moments with reverence. I embrace the Satori moments with joy.

And I am daring to step forth and shine, instead of hiding.

Going through all of this, I learned that I'm much stronger than I felt, braver than I believed, and smarter than I thought. I started to share the gifts and tools I discovered along the way, and as I did, people were getting insights and taking actions to change their own lives. I learned that I wasn't just an ambassador for Lifebook and Mindvalley, but in Life itself.

As for my beloved husband and I, our lives are totally different now. We decided to share our story with others in an effort to make a difference and to encourage others. We shared the tools we used to get through it. We opened up and stepped out of our comfort zone. It has allowed us to expand our community, and now we are part of a loving, united tribe of like minded people. It is glorious.

In the space of the unknown, there is the opportunity to explore as you learn what works, what doesn't, and how to find your own way. There is space to breathe, to dream, to just be. As you explore, you grow. You learn that the unknown doesn't take anything away from you, it opens you up to opportunities you didn't even know were there.

As a family, we created daily practices to keep us focused. Our intention as a family became making the most of our time spent together, and our relationships deepened. At dinner, we sit around and share our wins. In the evening, my beloved and I created a nightly ritual of healing, gratitude, and appreciation. My personal practice of compassion and gratitude expanded, giving me strength, helping me when things got challenging.

I discovered gifts within myself that I began to offer to the world. I have an ability to instantaneously create a meditation if someone gives me a word, feeling, or outcome. I dared to start practicing this skill with friends, and those who requested it. I helped people to see that meditation can be done in many ways, from the way you drink your tea, to a shift in breathing, to what you visualize, and even walking or the way you move your body. The power in the present moment, especially when in the space of the unknown, can make all the difference.

I was guiding people to dive deeper into what they really wanted in their lives, how to deal with the overwhelm of wanting to do it all by creating baby steps, how to create a daily practice to move them toward their vision. I stepped out of my shell to help others who were ready to move from surviving and just getting by to making the choice and taking action to thrive.

I wrote a story that was published. I started a business. I let my friend post some of the videos from the meditations that I offered others. I didn't worry about how I would look, I just wanted to give back to the world, to the community that had given so much to me.

All of this required me to step up and out of the shell I had created to keep me "safe". Events and meetings began to happen that changed my life in ways and directions I didn't expect. Small dreams started as thoughts, and somehow, someway, they began to manifest and come true. I learned the power of asking for help, instead of trying to do it all myself.

Here is the craziest part: none of this would have happened, if we hadn't experienced POEMS.

Pain is the compost
Creating the foundation
To grow if you choose.
~Dani Glaeser

Life will always have challenges. In the past, I ran from them. I did my best to avoid them. I wanted a life that was easy and breezy. I lived with the mindset of if I did this, then this would happen. I believed that if I got to a certain point then everything would be okay. And it never was the okay I had hoped for.

It was in the challenges and dealing with the hardships, which allowed me to discover my strength. I learned that the only thing I could change was me. I was the one who decided how I would respond in every single situation. That was where my strength was, in how I chose to respond. I chose to manage my anger, my fear, my emotions, to identify the triggers, explore why I felt triggered, and make different choices. I dove into my beliefs, looked at the ones that were limiting me, and made the decision to rewrite them.

As a result, I started to consciously choose the path less traveled. I learned how to listen, dared to make the choices that were harder than the others. I wanted growth. I embraced change.

It isn't always easy, but it's worth it.

Sharing our story has inspired others in ways we never imagined. We had hoped we could make a difference for others, not really thinking about the difference it would make for us. Since this happened, my beloved's diagnosis actually helped his first neurologist discover what was going on with one of his other patients. We've inspired other couples dealing with a diagnosis or a traumatic life shift.

I have changed. My beloved has changed. My children have changed. We have learned so much about ourselves, our family, our life, and our dreams. We see life in a new way.

We always have a choice. In that choice is power. It's up to us to decide if we want to empower ourselves, or give our power away. It's up to us to seek out the gifts and be open to opportunities. It's up to us to choose to focus on the past, present, or future. It's up to us to create a vision and aim for it. What choice will you make?

> *Our painful experiences aren't a liability—they're a gift.*
> *They give us perspective and meaning,*
> *an opportunity to find our unique purpose and our strength.*
> -Edith Eger

About the Author

When life throws you a curveball, how do you respond? When Dani's husband was diagnosed with POEMS Syndrome in 2018, after a year of neurological challenges, her world turned upside down. Her entire life shifted. As a result, Dani decided to become the founder of Inner Lighthouse Musings, which creates empowering experiences for those who need them. She has a particular interest in helping caregivers and their families.

Dani has spent the last five years being a caregiver to her husband and helping her family to thrive amidst the chaos with confidence and clarity. She is currently cultivating a community of support with the goal of inspiring and empowering others to live their best while being prepared for the worst. She noticed how important support and having some sense of certainty was to those having to revamp their lives while dealing with a long term illness, especially after treatment, when you aren't sure what "normal" means or what direction to head in after being focused on healing and coping.

Dani has spent the last twenty years leading and designing retreats, creating custom meditations, and doing motivational speaking for small groups. In the last five years, she and her family have been living the Lifebook Lifestyle, helping her husband recover his nerves, and she is now a certified Lifebook Leader, as well as Lifebook Ambassador for the Lifebook community.

This past year, she has been hosting monthly events for *Inner Freedom Outer Vision,* to help empower and inspire others. Dani has also contributed to the book *Soul Journey* that was published this year, and is in the process of working on two other books.

When Dani isn't writing or working on her business, you'll find her enjoying a cup of tea, journaling, cozied up with a good book, out for a walk, meditating (or creating one), hanging out with her family, or creating spaces of grace in the form of mini retreats from the chaos of today's world. She is a practitioner of gratitude and compassion, a lifelong learner, seeker of understanding, lover of tea, and promoter of self care.

Author Contact Info

Email: innerlighthousemusings.com

No matter how much falls on us,
we keep plowing ahead.
That's the only way to keep the roads clear.

~Greg Kincaid

Thriving After Surviving: How to Bounce Back and Strive Forward After Losing a Loved One to Suicide

by Jason Holzer

A gem cannot be polished without friction,
nor a man perfected without trials

~Lucius Annaeus Seneca

he beauty about being a parent is that your children will help you gain a new purpose. When my oldest son was born, I realized that it was time to become the best version of myself. In order to do that, I knew I needed to face my past and heal my wounds. Especially my wounds related to my father.

I knew this wouldn't be easy, but I was determined to create a new story for my family. Thus, I began the journey towards personal transformation and growth. It was time for me to win the game within, to master my mind and to follow the guidance of my soul. I had to do the work needed to be the father and husband I desired to be so that my wife and sons would never have to go through what I went through after I lost my Dad to suicide when I was only 17 years old.

Through the power of faith, reliance, and forgiveness, I now live a life on purpose, one filled with joy. I meet challenges with a positive mindset, and I use my story to inspire others to triumph over their trauma so that we can all become the very greatest versions of ourselves.

My father was a very gifted individual. He was a true craftsman, as well as a dedicated dad and husband. He was someone I truly looked up to as I grew up. I wanted to be like him in so many ways. He always knew how to make me laugh when I was having a rough day, and he was there to give me the tough love I needed when he knew I could do better. He was a phenomenal human being, and I loved him with all the love I had to give.

My father was always trying to make things better in every aspect of life. It didn't matter if it was something as big as our house or as small as my pinewood derby car in boy scouts, he always gave it his all. He had a mindset that anything could be improved. He worked diligently to provide for my mom, my sisters, and me. I never doubted his love and dedication to his family. I learned so many lessons about how to be a man and how to be a great human being from my father. His lessons have stayed with me throughout my life. For that, I am grateful.

As I was getting ready to turn 18, I really started to value my dad's opinion and perspective even more. I had gotten past the teen years where your parents just weren't that cool and realized that there was so much more my dad could teach me. I saw a man who had a purpose and a vision for his family and his career. It seemed like he had everything going for him externally.

It was what I couldn't see, though, that ended up changing the course of my life and my family member's lives forever. On May 8, 2003, my father passed away by suicide and left my family and me completely shattered. It was a day that started similar to one's previous, but it was a day that ended with feelings of deep pain, regret, confusion, abandonment, and the seemingly answerless question of "Why?"

I remember going from feeling every emotion possible all at once to feeling absolutely numb. I would feel lifeless at times, as I wondered how I could move forward after intense feelings of abandonment, confusion, anger, and sadness. Instead of allowing myself to feel and then heal, I consciously suppressed those feelings because I didn't want to embrace them, partly because they were so overwhelming at times.

However, whatever you consciously suppress eventually gets subconsciously expressed. I would have vivid dreams of being very angry with my dad, and they felt as if it was actually happening. I would wake up and it would take me twenty to thirty seconds to realize I was only dreaming. After this kept happening over and over again for a few years I started to question why these dreams were happening. I didn't want to be a resentful or angry person, but subconsciously that is how I felt. That is when I discovered journaling.

Through journaling, I was able to express my feelings of losing my dad and how it affected not only my life, but my family's lives as well. It was also through journaling where I would find inspiration and positivity. It felt as if God was sharing his plan for me through the pen and a pad. One of the first things I remember writing down was, "Forgive him."

Forgiveness was always something I learned about in school, but never understood the need for. Now, I knew I needed to forgive my dad because every time a significant life event happened, it was going to be a reminder that my dad would not be physically present. From my wedding to the birth of children, the moments that are supposed to be joyous and filled with excitement were also mixed with sadness. Thoughts of him not being there to celebrate my wedding, or knowing my sons will only experience their grandfather through pictures and stories, is a harsh and unfortunate reality. Practicing continuous forgiveness has helped me alleviate the heaviness of those harsh realities. I practiced forgiving my father, as well as forgiving myself for my difficult feelings all the years since his death.

Practicing forgiveness changed everything for me. It helped me realize that God is good and that he can turn any tragedy into triumph through practicing faith. He has given us free will to choose the direction of our lives and if we get in line with his plan for us, remarkable things start to happen. I made the decision to not be a victim of my circumstance and instead fight through the loss of my father by searching for God's plan in my own life.

I asked God for mentors and guidance, and God sent me an army of positive examples to show me how to live. They came in the form of family members, friends, and sometimes just a random connection. It is amazing how faithful God is to us when we are faithful to him. Every time I have questioned how I would get through a situation, I ask for guidance and if I keep an open mind, the way has always been shown to me.

God doesn't guarantee life will be easy, but He does guarantee it will be worth it. I had to make a choice to use my situation to help others who have also lost a loved one to suicide. I also decided that if I could prevent someone from going through what I went through by losing my dad to suicide, it would be worth it. However, it doesn't stop there, especially if we are willing and if we are able, it is actually just the beginning. The good news is all of us are able to do great things regardless of how big the task or the dream. My life's mission is to eliminate suicide through teaching mental prosperity and wellness.

It was the decision I made to flip the script and not be defined by a tragic loss that allowed me to create a better life for myself and for my family. I have learned that every failure is actually a step in the right direction with the right mindset and the right intent. I have become a student of myself, and I am constantly curious about why I am doing what I am doing and why I think the thoughts I think. The mind is a powerful tool, and we must learn how to control it or it will control us. Thinking is the most laborious work anyone can do, but it is also the most beneficial. When we truly understand what it means to think, our world starts to change.

When we build our self-image because we think of ourselves as someone who is loved, valued, and always enough, we become powerful beyond measure. There is no end to what we can do, the only end is the limiting thoughts that swirl in our head. It is like a governor on a student driver's car. Take the governor off and only see the possibilities. When you break down the word impossible it actually spells I'm possible. So even the roots of limiting vocabulary are actually limitless. The only thing stopping us from what we want is actually us. Believe we can achieve by knowing how to use our intellectual faculties which are our mental muscles.

For the most part, school teaches us about our five senses but rarely emphasizes our intellectual faculties. Then what happens is that we live our life based on what we can see, hear, taste, smell, and touch. What if I told you we were never meant to live that way, and that our senses are simply just to help us enjoy what it is we see on the inside?

Bob Proctor said it best when he said, " If you can see it in your mind, you can hold it in your hand." We live in a thought world. Everything around us started off as a thought and then through action became something we can see, hear, smell, taste, or touch. Our thoughts are what have shaped our current reality, and that is good news, because when we learn to change our thoughts, we start to change how we feel when we change how we feel, we change how we act, and then our results start to get better and better.

Everything we do has been conditioned through habits. A multitude of habits is called a paradigm. When we stack good habits, we build a paradigm that conditions us to continually do things that will benefit us. Whether it be exercising, eating healthy, managing tasks for the day, spending time with family, etc, it first starts with the discipline and willingness to do it, then simply continues to repeat over and over until it just becomes a part of who you are.

Let's take exercising for example. Everyone knows the benefits, but why don't they do it, or why do they stop after only a few weeks? It is because they have not identified themselves as someone who exercises. They have been temporarily motivated, and like the idea of being in better shape and having a healthier body, but they don't see themselves internally that way. The key is to form the idea in your mind that exercising then isn't necessarily something you do, it is who you are. When you identify yourself as an athlete, then you feel that internal drive to exercise, not the external motivation to make a short term change to only find yourself falling back into old habits.

When we learn to form your identity, we transform who we are into someone who is constantly growing. We also develop a sensical approach to fearlessness, which means we trust our intuition instead of our logic on whether or not something can be done. We can stretch ourselves beyond our limits because we have a high self-esteem and a positive self image.

A positive self image and believing in ourselves lead to becoming an elite optimist. An elite optimist doesn't wait for the light at the end of the tunnel, instead they are the light through the tunnel. They know that regardless of what happens to them in life, they will eventually find something positive from the experience they go through. For me personally, it took over a decade after I lost my father to suicide to figure out how I could ever find something positive from something so tragic. However, I clung to my faith and believed that life will eventually get better. Now almost twenty years later, I am able to see nearly all situations as something training me and preparing me to fulfill my purpose in life. There are still challenging moments, especially as a parent, but as the great writer Rumi says, "Oh ye who can't take a good rub, how will you ever become a polished gem?"

Becoming an elite optimist doesn't mean everything goes our way all the time, but it does mean that we are quick to find the meaning and the lesson in this experience we call life. As we go through life, it's important to remember the phrase coined by Srikumar Rao, "Good thing, bad thing, who knows," as we go through life's journey. Let's delay the label and let things play out before we judge circumstances. This is especially true if we believe that all circumstances are gifts and opportunities. Magic happens when we can train our minds to search for and find the gifts and opportunities in any situation.

Finally, you become humbly confident, which means you stand in our truth, but at the same time realize that everyone knows something you don't. This allows your imagination to flourish and only see what is possible. Competition doesn't interest you anymore, because you have become a creator and you lift others up around you. Samuel "Golden Rule" Jones said it best, "What I want for myself, I also want for everyone else." Reach new heights, and be sure to help others do the same. In the end, life is about what you can give when you know the other can't give back, because you understand the great secret of life.

A positive self image and believing in ourselves
lead to becoming an elite optimist.
An elite optimist doesn't wait for the light at the end of the tunnel,
instead they are the light through the tunnel.
~Jason Holzer

About the Author

Growing up in Taos, Missouri, Jason was raised in a small town with a loving family that gave him every chance to succeed. His parents were supportive and provided everything this 17-year-old could ever want. That is, until his life changed forever on May 8, 2003, when his dad unexpectedly passed away by suicide, leaving him, his mother, and two younger sisters behind.

Through hard work, dedication, and a strong faith in God, Jason is now a certified teacher, an accomplished basketball and mental fitness coach and Post-Traumatic growth storyteller. He is passionate about sports, and co-founded 4D Athletes to bring conscious coaching into the world.

He is committed to personal growth, his marriage and family, athletics, suicide prevention, and creating WIN-WIN relationships. Jason is able to handle multiple projects with strong follow through. He is reliable, inspired, and organized, and feels equally comfortable as a leader or as a team player. Jason has a keen empathy towards others and is committed to helping create positive change in the world.

Jason coaches to empower people to master their minds and win the game with compassion, grit and authenticity. His vision is to bring mindset and peak performance into the world of sports. He envisions a world where his company, 4D Athletes, creates people who are confident, self-motivated, and empowered. Athletes of all ages will talk about how 4D Athletes prepared them for life and to have the courage to follow their path in life. With life transforming content, events and training; 4D Athletes creates a shift in sports where winning in life becomes the priority which leads to winning on the scoreboard.

Jason is married to his lovely wife Mary and is the father of two amazing sons. They are the source of his inspiration and they help him become better every single day.

Author Contact Information

Email: jasonholzer6@gmail.com
Website: www.jasonholzer.com

Rise of the Phoenix

by Kanika Jain

I can be changed by what happens to me.
But I refuse to be reduced by it.

~Maya Angelou

n difficult times, heroes are made!

Quite the cliché to start with, isn't it? However, this is exactly how my life turned out to be. So, let's dive in as I excitedly take you through the journey of how I became a true heroine of my life.

I grew up with humble beginnings in a family of four consisting of my parents and my elder sister on a tiny island in the Middle East called Bahrain. We were simple in our living with a traditional-modern family set up intertwining our Indian values and traditions with a per se Western outlook of raising independent children. My dad placed education first, as it was paramount for him to make us self-sufficient in life apart from giving us a certain amount of freedom to do what we liked including pursuing our hobbies. We weren't as financially abundant as we are today, so asking for anything always came with a mental disclaimer of value for money. I could see how tirelessly my dad tried to create a wonderful life for us, and my mother worked to meet the budgets of the household expenses. We were not deprived of anything, we just didn't have a lot to spend on luxury items at that time."

My mother always inculcated values of being loving, respectful and kind to others, helping anyone in need and speaking the truth- the basic values I uphold to this day. However, we did go by some societal rules due to family pressures such as religious beliefs of not touching holy idols while menstruating, girls getting married when they reach 25 years, it was as if a girl's life was all about compromise. The biggest one was never to question the elders as it was a mark of disrespect.

These were the things that panicked me, as they honestly really did not make sense and were contradictory to my belief system. Confining me and my thoughts were like chaining my free spirit that wanted to just enjoy and live meaningfully.

I always strived to be the perfect daughter in every possible way right from getting perfect grades in school to listening to everything my parents told me, which sometimes even extinguished certain desires that I had.

My schooling years had so much drama that I could create a show on TV narrating it. I was fat shamed as an overweight kid and deemed as the pimply girl in my teenage years. This followed my first ever heartbreak and getting shunned by girls just because I finally lost the weight and now was the popular girl among the guys. Jealousy and backbiting were the themes during my high school years. However, the strange part was, that never did all this belittling ever dim my light. As a matter of fact, it made me stronger and exposed me to standing for injustice and bullying at a younger age. I knew I had something in me that was ready for a much greater life, I just didn't know what it was due to all this noise.

Just when I was happy that school and its drama was done and I now get to enjoy university life in a different country, the universe presented me with another pandora's box. This included a massive culture shock of living in the UK. The lies and betrayal from friends, peer pressures of drinking alcohol, receiving contraceptives on my orientation day, yes, I saw a condom for the first time, entering a casino, I literally witnessed it all. It was super overwhelming but made me understand life better. Also, I must applaud my parents for grounding in me such strong values that these things didn't sway me into ways that would be detrimental in any manner.

After university, came excelling at work and getting promotions. Like a good girl I kept on ticking the boxes of the so called "rulebook of life" one after the other, slowly killing the true spirit within me until the time when I finally got my major kick from life. Many times, we are faced with situations in life that are the biggest wake up calls that we ever need. That, my friends is what happened to me.

It was May 2018; I got into a toxic marriage that completely drained me not only physically but emotionally and mentally before ending in exactly 19 days. Yes, you heard it right, 19 days. One would think what worse could have happened in just a couple of days, but long story short, I was a victim of not just lies and deceptions but also greed. My husband at that time was wearing a façade, paid little to no attention to me, was emotionally distant from me and lied about some big areas of his life such as his financial status, his job etc.

Most days I stayed alone in a small dingy flat devoid of any human connection with my daily meals comprising of just red kidney beans, cereals, and bananas. Soon, my mind fogged with immense negativity and my health started deteriorating. My husband didn't even take me to the hospital, instead he poisoned me and when I rebelled, I was taken down with a couple of pills.

After a lot of heated discussions to go back home to my parents, I finally flew back all shattered in a wheelchair, as I could not even walk properly. I was immediately taken to the doctor and diagnosed as massively malnourished with five different illness and was put on ten pills per day for the next 45 days to recover physically.

With the unconditional love and care of my family, my condition started improving. However, I still felt so shallow. My health was not ramping up and conditions relapsed. My mind was just crammed with negative thoughts and vengeance, my heart aching and crying each day as I woke up feeling betrayed by life. A happy independent soul living a so-called perfect life in her dictionary finally endured her biggest of what some call the dark night of the soul. However, I like to call it my "Beautiful Destruction".

> *Sometimes in life you have to destroy what is merely good,*
> *to allow what is truly great to come in.*
> -Vishen Lakhiani

The nature of life is as such that certain things must fall apart massively for a greater piece to emerge. As in my case, I went through the worst dip of my life to transform into a butterfly ready to fly, see and feel the world in her own extraordinary way. Coming back, fed up with how things were moving in an absolutely depressing trajectory in my life, I finally thought of taking matters in my hand and prayed to God to show me a tiny step that I can take with the hope to better my life. Just then the Universe heard my calling. Heard of the saying "ask and you shall receive"? That happened instantly for me.

I clearly remember that night, as I was gazing and looking at myself in the mirror with my teary eyes all dejected, my inner voice slowly whispered, "You Are Power." I looked perplexed to see who that was when the soulful whisper reiterated the same thing. Physiologically, I felt tingles all over my body when I heard that. It was exhilarating yet confusing. Continuing to ponder over that whisper, I mindlessly opened Instagram to see the first thing that popped up was a Masterclass from Mindvalley (MV) with Vishen and Marisa Peer. It was strange how I instantly felt a sense of hope when they both spoke on how the mind listens to everything we say. I felt skeptical but deep down it's as if I knew truth in what they were explaining.

This led to me devouring one free masterclass after another, with different authors and topics which in its own way boosted my morale and made me understand that I had the opportunity to change my life if I wished to do so. The claims in each masterclass were so big and groundbreaking that my logical brain could not understand how life can turn out so amazing. I decided to take the challenge to try bending my own reality and truly took the best decision of my life. I now know that I lit the spark within me once again and released the true free spirit that I had locked up in a box for so long. I refused to indulge in self-pity anymore and took the director's seat in my life where I held the reins with my own hands. I was committed to breaking down all that didn't serve me.

The phoenix had indeed risen with her wings spread to soar even higher. My first main goal was to focus on my health and ditch the conventional medical treatment I was being given. I still remember my first purchase was the Wildfit quest.

What that did to me and my body in a span of 3 months was astonishing. I got to a healthier version of my body to the extent that I even corrected an auto-immune disease and chucked those pills out. Yes!! This attracted me more to MV. My next purchase was Marisa Peers Rapid Transformational Hypnotherapy. One can only imagine when you rewire your brain not just for vibrant health, wealth, relationships but abundance in every form as well, there is no stopping you. I kept working not only on my body but recoding my mind and my belief system, slowly uprooting my limiting beliefs. It was indeed a paradigm shift! Tearing down the scarcity mindset in so many areas of my life gave me much more clarity and ignited a sense of purpose within me. I was convinced that I was no longer going to play small, and I had a strong desire to help people through the realizations I had witnessed during my journey.

I kept on immersing myself extensively in areas ranging from attaining a better body and mindset, to career growth and relationships building and development to honing my entrepreneurial abilities. MV was nothing less than my very own guardian angel who entered my life at the right moment.

I also started interacting greatly with the amazing tribe on the platform consisting of incredible souls from all around the globe coming from different walks of life. I kept on meeting people who made me push my own boundaries in every way possible. They shared vulnerably, encouraged, and cheered for me, inspired me, and became my friends for life. I made deep connections even during the covid pandemic and had a circle that I used to look forward to connecting with. This tribe not only motivated me to follow my path and purpose, but also appreciated me for who I am and how far I have come.

This little girl from Bahrain who was unrecognizable truly became recognized and loved for who she truly is. I started learning directly from other personal transformation authors learning tools, and practicing them on myself daily and igniting those dormant talents within me one at a time.

By 2021, little did I know that I became a personal growth junkie, taking my transformation so super seriously, that it became an inherent component of my life. While doing the "3 Most Important Questions"- a potent tool from Vishen Lakhiani, I still remember that it was the first time I dreamt big. I wanted to:

- Be in top masterminds connecting with world class leaders and changemakers.
- Be an educator changing the current broken education system
- Be super fit, learning and teaching different modalities relating to nutrition and holistic health.
- Be an inspirational speaker who coaches others.
- Live and enjoy the rich life with my family.
- Learn the art of speaking and build deep connections.
- Go to amazing educational festivals to better myself exponentially.

The list goes on. I wrote all this and much more down in the winters of 2018 not knowing that out of the combined 26 items of experiences, growth, and contributions that I had listed, I would meet 85% of them by 2022! Wow!!! Time to update this list with yet another mind-blowing upgraded list of my moonshots and 10X dreams.

When I did a reverse gap analysis of my life while studying to be a health coach, I realized all the major dips in my life had happened to bring me into this moment in time. To make me ready for who I am today and who I am embodying as I create my future on my terms. Those life lessons and challenges were mere obstacles to clear off beliefs that were stopping and blocking me to achieve my dreams and a life that I truly deserve.

Epiphanies after epiphanies followed in my transformation journey with many realizations and teachings. Here are some especially for you.

Be who you want to be, throwing out the thought of judgment from others in your backyard. Even if you want to be a home maker, it doesn't even matter! Sometimes we really put tags on things deeming them as insignificant, while everything in life has its own meaning and importance. I know my mother is a homemaker and it takes courage, love, and consistency to do a job daily where you aren't paid and your family may at times take you for granted.

Understand your talents and natural gifts. This takes time but it stems from going deep and knowing your core personality and value system, that is, what you do best and where you're able to make your best contributions. Ask yourself- what do you genuinely enjoy and love doing without any stress? It's the work that lights you up naturally. Try honing them rather than focusing on your weakness.

There is always a solution to tackle your weaknesses- Delegate to those who love doing the work you don't. Not being true to yourself is the biggest disservice in life. It's like going to a masquerade party with a mask on. At one point you will feel suffocated leading you to throw that mask away (that's what burnout feels like). There is a unique essence when you show up as your true self each day.

Make your dream list and start working towards it one baby step at a time. I believe the word "dreams" excites us more than the word "goals". Start asking yourself what would my dream life look like? How would I be and feel at the end of this year if I were to live my dream life. Look into that life in details and feel every bit of it.

Embrace the discomfort that comes with achieving your dreams. Understand the blocks that are limiting you. Question yourself on how these blocks have already hindered you for not taking action towards your dreams. Remember, the closer you get to your goals, the more your fear intensifies. It's because your ego is not in tandem and wants to safeguard itself from any drastic change that moves you out of our comfort zone. You should get a little bit excited about the fact that you're feeling this fear, because it means a remarkable breakthrough is near.

Don't be afraid to fail.

Relationships matter. Give quality time to your loved ones. Your family is your invisible support system. Let them know how much you love them, and that they matter. My family time is that one time slot where I bask in unconditional love, care, and feel alive.

Create a circle of like-minded exponential souls that inspire you to stretch and get bolder in life, pick you up when you feel low and show you your innate potential, and how to unleash and shine it even more. Bounce off ideas to co-create wonderful things with them. Moreover, they check up on me if I vanish from their hindsight. This piece was a game changer for me as I realized that we are community made not self-made. We need support in life.

Start investing in yourself and stay dedicated to it. Get mentors and coaches.Read books that empower you and fills your soul. Do courses that make you better and hone your gifts even further. Ask for help when needed. You cannot do everything alone in life. Trust me, this piece of self- learning is one of the best commitments I made for my abundant life.

There's a unique magic when you start developing yourself consciously in different areas of your life. It becomes a positive addiction as you are amazed by how much you can learn and transform. Positively working on one area causes a ripple effect on other areas too as they are all interdependent. However, focuson one area first, be monomaniacally invested in it, and as you start to notice encouraging tangible transformations that you feel complete with, move to the next. This will help to reduce the overwhelming feeling of doing it all at once and gives you the opportunity of enjoying your journey.

Be spiritual and acknowledge there is a higher power above supporting you. Acknowledge that you are a fractal of the source witnessing earth and the human experience. The universe will only give you what you are capable of handling even if you don't think this way in a given moment.

Be a constant learner just like a child, in a state of continual awe and curiosity. You can seriously learn from anyone or any opportunity.

Never lose the sparkle in your eyes and your sense of wonder about the things most people take for granted.

Deliver your craft with love and happiness always. My friend bakes only cookies for a living, but she bakes the best cookies as she creates every batch from her heart. The moment I bite in, I can taste and feel not just the gooeyness of the cookies, but the smell of her love and care. Whatever you deliver know that it will be felt by each soul you touch and change their life in a beautiful manner.

Leave people better than how you met them. Do everything that lifts your frequency and mood up every day so that you can pull people up with you.

Always pay it forward from your heart with the best of the intentions without expecting any reward from it.

Today, I can proudly say that I'm not only a certified holistic health coach but a certified quantum healer, quantum flow practitioner, entrepreneur, author, and a speaker living out my dreams and purpose one baby step at a time, whilst continually evolving myself into the next layer of my being. If someone told me all this back in 2018, I would never believe it.

I wake up each day consciously deciding to create the life that I wish to live, helping and serving people in the best way possible. Sure, I may have some soft blows some days but that's the part of a human experience. I live with no regrets, as I understand that whatever is the outcome of my actions in life, whether good or bad, there is always an embedded lesson or a blessing for me. It's so soul filling to walk through life in this fashion.

By now you must be thinking that this is like a typical fairy tale, but fairy tales narrated by Disney movies are quite constrained and linear in their thoughts.

My story dear one is a rollercoaster of phenomenal life adventures and challenges which may be excruciatingly difficult, but at the end all I can say is, it was a ride well taken and truly enriching.

> *To be yourself in a world that is constantly trying*
> *to make you something else is the greatest accomplishment.*
> -Ralph Waldo Emerson

Life is indeed beautiful, sometimes sweet, sometimes messy, sometimes painful, and sometimes incredible. The more you open up, the more you understand that we are mere actors on this amazing stage of life, and we get to shape and change our characters in it our own way if we choose to do so.

My invitation for you is to take an additional half-hour each day to treat yourself better, educate and love yourself, relax in your favorite way and reaffirm what an awesome person you are. In the end, it all works out if you are willing to do the work for yourself.

IF I CAN DO IT, YOU CAN TOO!!

So, if you ask me, what does it take to be a "Hero"? To me being a "Hero" is to have that courage and commitment to show up each day knowing that whatever life throws onto your path, you will handle that curveball and ignite yourself with that burning desire of doing what your souls truly wants to. Know that we are always a work in progress, ready to take uncomfortable actions required in the moment for us to evolve. We repurpose our personal pains and challenges from the past to create massive offerings of pure service for others. Be intentional each day about the life we wish to create not only for us but for the collective. I passionately believe that I can only perform and serve at my highest potential if I constantly learn and upgrade myself. Ahh what a journey it has been!

For me, my mantra in life is "Evolve Consciously & Authentically".

So, how do you want to live your life? Loving it or merely Living it?

All my love,
Kanika

About the Author

Kanika Jain is a Holistic Health Coach, Quantum Healer, Quantum Flow Practitioner and a Chartered Financial Analyst (CFA). She loves to empower people to know and love themselves, equipping them with tools to live meaningful & radiant lives, propelling them to realize their own inner power to "evolve consciously and authentically.

Author Contact Information

Email: kanika.j6@gmail.com
Instagram: kanikajain.love
Facebook: https://www.facebook.com/kanika.jain.92317

You Are the Seed That Has All You Need for Your Best Life

by Brynn Jordan

*I've come to believe that each of us has a personal
calling that's as unique as a fingerprint,
that the best way to succeed is to discover what you love,
and then find a way to offer it to others in
the form of service, working hard,
and also allowing the energy of the universe to lead you.*

~Oprah Winfrey

here is a theory out there that our souls choose the life we get to live on the earth plane. There are lessons to learn and experiences to experience to expand the all-knowing and all intelligent spiritual field. Well, if that is true, then my soul was not messing around with its choice. To be honest, there are days I am rather "pissed off" with my soul for choosing the experiences I have had to go through from the age of five years old.

My childhood was what my therapists call traumatic! I have learnt that trauma comes in many forms. Mine was primarily mental and emotional trauma caused by so much confusion and scariness for the world around me. In addition to all that, I also had a once off physical sexual abuse encounter as a five year-old with a man, a complete stranger when I was on holiday with my family. So there's been a lot of lessons for me to experience in this life I have chosen.

I was born into a coloured family in a small town in Apartheid South Africa. Coloured in South Africa means mixed race (26% UKI, 25% Indian, 9% Xhosa, 8% Bantu Balance, too many to mention according to my DNA tests). When I was growing up, ideas like an abundance mindset and feeling worthy were never discussed nor passed down to me. I believe it is generational, since I come from a bloodline of people who felt not worthy simply for the sin of their skin color. We were considered less just because we weren't white. We were denied education, vital skills, and support for attaining good lives.

The main thing I was taught during school was to be fearful, to comply with any rules a white person gave me no matter if it was right or wrong, and to always know my place. I was taught early on that I must always dim my light to stay under the radar! I didn't want to attract any attention for many reasons. The most important of which was that I was gender non-conforming from birth, as well as being gay in a community of Christians with limited education on dealing with differences kindly. And that's me being kind in the way I am describing it. It was a rough, dark time for me.

Life felt like a prison for as long as I could remember as a kid. I constantly felt cursed! I constantly felt wrong at my core! I constantly felt a pain in my heart.

I grew up having complete strangers walk up to me in the street and they would give me their unsolicited opinions on what a freak I was, what a joke I was and what a shame I was to the human race. I heard many, many hurtful and heavy things during my childhood. It felt like I would hear these taunts every time I stepped out of my family home to face the world. I lived in fear and I lived in shame.

During high school, I decided to adopt Oprah Winfrey as my spirit Mom and Nelson Mandela as my spirit Dad. And at that time I had no idea why, but looking back I realized that I saw a light in them. I saw how they were able to rise above all life had thrown at them and re-write the rules to become inspiring people. They had been able to see things differently and were very committed to the calling they heard, despite the world telling them to the contrary. I could never explain this to anyone when I was sixteen years old, but I just knew that my life would be significantly different. I just had no idea how. Oprah and Madiba reached me by shining their light bright and I wanted to do the same. That was the gift Oprah and Madiba gave me and wow, did more magic start to unfold from that point on.

What I know for sure is that life is full of *magic*, and we as humans are also filled with so much *magic*. There is definitely something to this "Soul" having a Human Experience and how we are all connected to each other in so many profound ways. There is something bigger, wiser, loving, supportive, and collective that connects us all. My adopting Oprah and Madiba as my soul parents are an example of this. The younger me lived purely on instinct on some very big turning points in my life that kept fine tuning the trajectory of my life to being the best it could be.

And what is my life today, you may ask?

Well, I am a proud and out gender non-binary being who loves men, and I am able to express that in my daily life, in all my important relationships, my family, and in my professional life and communities. Not many marginalized people get to live like I do, and I realize that. I am grateful that I am really free to be myself and that I am free to prosper!

After many years of fear and sadness, I finally know what self-love feels like, what love feels like, and that brings me peace in my heart. I make more money than I can spend and I even make money in my sleep! Life constantly presents me with opportunities to learn and grow and thrive despite some of my mistakes. Life has unfolded in ways beyond my wildest dreams. I have traveled the world, met people from all over the globe, created deep rewarding relationships with amazing people, and best of all, I have experienced the lightness of forgiving people. Each day, I am able to look in the mirror and smile softly and beautifully at the person that I am today. I have so much choice at my fingertips that life really does feel full and blessed more consistently than ever.

I have been down as far as you could imagine, and I was able to rise above it all with some amazing tools which have made a huge difference in my life. The main tool I use is developing my intuition. It has made the biggest difference to me being my best and living my best life!

If there is anything to take away from my story, it is that you can develop your intuition and hone it by working on these three areas that will transform your life beyond your wildest dreams:

1. *Higher States:* Your intuition is the language of the soul! Invest, grow, and develop this language to open a communication channel to the best magic the universe can offer anyone.
2. *Awareness*: Find a way to reflect, take stock, and grow awareness of the unfolding in this earth plane by practicing gratitude. As long as you develop a way to stop, smell the roses, and connect the dots, the universe will find ways to speak to you. It helps if you agree on some language frameworks with the universe, so it becomes unique to you. Maybe it's in signs you see around you or messages you are receiving, whichever way it comes, be ready to listen and be grateful.
3. *Learning:* Evolve, expand, and grow with the Universe. It is constantly expanding, enriching, and experiencing deeper and greater. As you exist within such an ever-expanding universe, keep up by growing and expanding yourself! It is quite a good way to avoid "pain" being your teacher.

Your Intuition is the Language of The Soul / Magic / Universe

Intuition to me is the language of Vibration, Frequency, and Energy. It can be difficult to always put intuition into descriptive words, but it is so clear to us when it is felt. I also know that intuition is like a muscle and to get muscles strong and working well for you, you need to put the muscle to work. Invest in it, develop it, put in consistent exercise, and nurture it. I sometimes find the laws of life powerfully simple with a touch of annoyance. Yes, I said it! A touch of annoyance. This is true though; you will always get what you put into something. Life is all about giving and receiving. It remains a timeless dance and consistent truth of Energy and strengthening your Intuition.

In my professional world where I consult to the globe's top CFOs (Chief Financial Officers) and Finance communities, I am finding the growing need for creativity, empathy, and intuition in the corporate workplace. Part of my management consulting gig is to help my clients unleash higher performance in their organizations and human ingenuity at the intersection of technology, business performance, and innovation. Technology is advancing at such a pace that all left-brain type work is being matched and done by digital workers / artificial intelligence versus a human being. The call to bring heart-centeredness, empathy, and intuition to the workplace is becoming more significant than ever today. That is setting apart people from the masses of commoditized skills.

There will be greater need for those people that can access higher wisdom, intelligence, empathy, and insights beyond the logical. People with missions / callings are changing the world, the workplace, and their communities. Intuition plays a significant role in all of this, and weaves together all the unleashing of the magic on the world to make it better.

What has really moved the dial for me on the intuition front are the following tools and techniques. These techniques can be categorized across these broad areas, as stated above:

1. *Higher States:* Connecting to higher States of wisdom and intelligence through meditation, muscle testing, and journaling.
2. *Awareness:* Developing and sustaining your own intuition through learning to listen to the language of the universe via symbolism and cues from the universe to raise your awareness.
3. *Learning:* Continuously growing and evolving yourself by learning from teachers, gurus, and those around you to learn new systems of effectiveness in health, finances, higher performance, spirituality, etc.

Connecting to Higher States of Wisdom and Intelligence and Tuning In to Intuition

Meditation

I know meditation can be so cliché, but it really does work. There has been so much research around just how good meditation is for your being and happiness. In the past, it was believed that our brains actually declined as we age, however there is a growing body of research showing that actually, the brain can form new pathways, thus creating new ways of thinking and being. This is the idea of neuroplasticity, and it is exciting because it means that you can change your brain! Mediation is one of the ways that you can create these new connections in your brain.

Meditation also helps you get much more cohesion between the left and right brain, which takes your creativity and consciousness to another level. Give me some of that please, and keep it coming for my best life! Meditation has truly been a game changer for me and I have learned many different types of mediation. The most effective meditations for me are ones that allow me to open up to receive information from the universe, and which allows me to level up my consciousness. I also love active meditation techniques, which I will describe below.

Meditation to Level Up Consciousness

This technique is the meditation I use the most and I absolutely love it. I learned this through Emily Fletcher, who created the Ziva technique. Now there is a whole process to go through to get into a rhythm, but essentially you learn how to go through the phases of Mindfulness, Meditation, and Manifestation through the Ziva technique. I have adapted it slightly so it works for my lifestyle needs.

You Are the Seed That Has All You Need for Your Best Life

This is my adapted process:

- Get into position for meditation, which could be sitting in a chair or sitting cross legged on a bed. At all times, make sure that your back is supported, and that your neck is free and not supported.
- Start with some simple breath work by inhaling for 2 counts, exhaling for 4 counts two times, then inhaling for 3 counts, exhaling for 6 counts two times, and finally, inhaling for 4 counts and exhaling for 8 counts two times.
- I then introduce some active meditation techniques mostly learned from Jeffrey Allen:
  - Ground yourself and the room for a few minutes by imagining a root growing out from your root chakra (by the bottom of your torso) and let the root grow deep into the earth. Send any worries, challenges, or what is on your mind at the time down this root into Mother Earth, which can take and support whatever you send down.
  - Turn down your analyzer. This is that little voice in your head. Imagine a switch in your head, and turn down the volume of analyzing to zero.
  - Move to a higher space of consciousness by imagining being in the center of your head, and then going up from that center point a bit, and then further back in your head. That is the sweet spot for your higher consciousness.
- Now, allow the mantra to come forward and repeat it over and over for about 17 minutes. (A mantra is a word or sound you repeat like Om, Just This, Here/Now). You can use a time keeping device in front of you to keep track of time. It is advised not to set alarms to time yourself, rather start training your body and mind to know how long 19 minutes feels. 19 minutes being the 17 minutes of meditation plus the 2 minutes for initial mindfulness stuff.
- Listen for an answer. This is a technique I learned from Michael Beckwith's teachings. During the meditation phase, you can be in the energy of listening, as if you are listening for an answer from someone who is very wise. Stay in the energy of listening for

something important while doing the meditation. Remember, the answer might come in that meditation or later in the day.

- Once the 19 minutes are done, move into the Manifestation phase of the meditation for about 2 to 3 minutes. In most cases I do a technique called segmentation, which is basically imagining my perfect day. I would divide my day into key blocks of time and then imagine the best experience or outcome for that block of time. Other techniques I use here include:
    - Gratitude practices (I usually do this for my evening meditation).
    - Imagining and feeling in the moment / outcome for any other manifestations I want in my life.

Some key points to consider for making this practice truly effective:

- You will never get away from thoughts coming and going in your mind! Think of yourself at a party and your guest of honor is the mantra. Simply introduce them to the thought, say your hellos and move onto something else. Just always try to come back to the Mantra.
- There are various Mantras out there, research for Mantras that resonate with you.
- To truly see the benefits, you must do this practice twice a day.
- Also consider fixing the two slots a day and replace them with the type of meditation that works for your life needs. Some days might need more active meditations and others more leveling up consciousness.

Active Meditation Technique

Active meditation is using the power and wisdom of higher states of consciousness to get you inspired answers, or an inspired way forward on any topic you may have. There are so many options in this category. The one that has really made the difference for me is the Silva Method by Jose

Silva. This can be incredibly useful for manifestations, problem-solving, as well as just for some good old inspiration, which I like to think of as the voice of the soul.

There are two parts to this kind of meditation. The first one is getting into an Alpha state, which is getting your brain to be at the frequency of Alpha. Believe it or not, we all have this ability to get our brains to an alpha state, and this is where all the magic happens. And then you move into the manifestation part of it, where you work with the alpha state to envision that which you want to create.

Here is a basic framework for this kind of meditation:

Getting to Alpha State

- Get into position for meditation either by sitting on a chair or cross legged on your bed or any other comfortable place. Make sure that your back is supported and that your neck is free and unsupported.
- Imagine the number three that flashes three times in front of you.
- Start with relaxing every part of your body from head to toe. So go from scalp, to forehead, to eyes, nose, cheeks, mouth, neck, shoulders, upper arms, lower arms, chest, abdomen, hips, thighs, calves, feet, and toes. Simply relax each body part.
- Now imagine the number two flashing three times in front of you.
- Then move into relaxing your mind. Imagine being in your favorite nature spot and taking in that scenery for a while.
- Now imagine the number 1 flashing three times in front of you.
- Then move into counting down from ten to zero and allowing yourself to go deeper into your consciousness.
- You now have reached alpha state.

Working with Alpha State

- For manifesting, I use the three scenes technique:
  - First, get into the Alpha state, as described above.
  - Then imagine a mental screen a few meters in front of you.

- ○ Start with scene number one.
- ○ Then project your challenge / project you would like to solve or execute.
- ○ Feel the pain of the challenge and make the colors brighter.
- ○ Feel the negative emotions and suffering you want to remove from your life.
- ○ Exaggerate these emotions and truly feel them.
- ○ Stop, and then move the mental screen 15 degrees to the left to move to Scene number 2.
- ○ Imagine you are now taking baby steps to solve the challenge or execute the project.
- ○ Make the colors brighter, use your senses to feel and see who is around you, what do you hear? Where are you? What do you smell? What do you feel taking these baby steps?
- ○ Stop, and then move the screen 15 degrees to the left and move into Scene number 3.
- ○ Imagine this challenge is being solved or the project has an outcome.
- ○ How do you feel? How are you celebrating?
- ○ See how this benefits other people having this challenge resolved or project outcome achieved.
- ○ Keep imagining the colors as bright as possible.
- ○ Count yourself out of the meditation from 5 to 1.

The more you practice getting to Alpha state the easier it will become to get into that state. There are some practices where you can programme in a symbol, which could be for example your thumb and index finger touching. So as you practice the full relaxation cycle, you have your index finger and thumb touching to trigger your alpha process. In the future you could get into alpha state in seconds, and go straight into the active meditation techniques simply by using the physical technique of touching your thumb and index finger to invoke your Alpha state.

Muscle testing is another way to enhance your intuition. This can be an independently useful way to get to the bottom line of what you are feeling or thinking. There are various ways one can do self-muscle testing. The one I have found the most reliable is the one using my arms.

Self-muscle test technique:

- Form an L shape with your dominant arm in front of you. Keep it close to your body.
- Place your hand from your non-dominant arm on your wrist of the dominant arm.
- Now do a test, e.g "Give me a yes" and push down with your non-dominant arm on your dominant arm while resisting the push from your dominant arm. This will hold firm.
- Do a test on "Give me a no" and push down with your non-dominant arm on your dominant arm while resisting the push from your dominant arm. Your dominant arm will not be able to hold firm.
- You can do extra true and false statements to double check such as; My name is (your real name) and My name is (a false name).
- Then ask the question you would like an answer for and note your result.

Muscle testing has been useful for me to check in with myself or as an extra validation of what my intuition is feeling. I found this very complementary in helping me strengthen my intuition. My strong recommendation is play with this and build up a trust between yourself and the wisdom of your body. I have found this useful in the following scenarios in combination with my intuitive prompts:

- Confirming an emotion I am feeling.
- Checking if an action is good for my well-being, inner peace, and happiness.
- Checking if anything I will consume is good for me or not.
- Checking if I have released negative emotions and energy.

Journaling

Finally, in the intuition space is journaling. It remains the most effective way to get clarity on what you really are feeling in your heart of hearts. It is a way to get what you are thinking out of your mind and into reality to make sense of it. The two most useful techniques I use include writing at least three pages of consciousness streaming first thing in the morning before I meditate. You will be amazed with what starts forming when you free flow with this type of journaling.

The other technique that helps is writing my dialogue between myself and my higher self. It helps to give your higher self a name. Simply writing out the dialogue between yourself and your higher self will give you access to answers that are already inside you that come from that all knowing, very wise part of you. What is awesome about this is that you can have any discussion on any topic with your higher self.

Awareness: Growing Your Awareness To The Unfolding Of Your Life

Intuition is the big foundation for your best life. Everything else feeds off of that. It is the major connection to all things wise, intelligent, and inspired. I have always enjoyed tapping into my intuition, but the fun really began for me when I realized I could create my own unique language with the Universe to get clear feedback, clear messages, and clear inspired actions from the Universe. This is all about co-creating with the Universe, and giving permission for the Universe to have full on conversations with you.

Symbolism is the most powerful technique for me. It is a way for the Universe to get my attention or raise my awareness to something I need to note. What has been useful is agreeing what these symbols mean with the Universe, and then simply letting go until they show up. An example of this is that I personally use butterflies as my symbol for the universe to communicate all things that have to do with relationships to me. I use ladybugs as the symbol for any key manifestation inspired action, and rainbows are symbols to me for the times that the Universe reminds me it has my back especially, especially for times when I get into some dark spaces in my head when it comes to life. I go one step further by putting these symbols on my Vision Boards, which helps me connect the dots when the Universe does show me the inspiration.

The fun and magic really begins to happen when you start seeing these symbols show up in the most surprising places. I have had symbols and messages come to me in the form of relevant quotes sent to me by family and friends that have a rainbow or butterfly in the background. I once met a man with a butterfly tattoo on the back of his hand and had a simple prompt from my intuition to get to know him. That was one of the most healing and enlightening conversations I have had with a man, and this was right around the time I was doing some work on healing my relationship to masculinity. The messages can come from anywhere, so be awake and aware!

I love numbers and I use 44 or 444 as the "Universal Yes" symbol. When I am at a crossroads and I see those numbers, I know it is a sign leading me the way I need to go. That is exactly how I got my dream house. I was out on a run when I had an intuitive flash to enter a nearby housing estate. I saw a house for sale and decided to check it out. The instruction at the gate to the estate said to dial house number 8 and when the person answered, they said the house for sale was actually number 44. I was so surprised, but I knew it was a message so I listened. The rest is history, as I now live in one of the best neighborhoods with no traffic to anywhere I want to go. I love my home, and I love having incredible get-togethers at my house, filling it with love, light, and laughter. I often catch myself smiling and in those moments, I take a moment and thank my house for all the amazing energy I get to feel daily living in it. The Universe did all the work and got me the perfect home.

Just be clear with the Universe how you want information, and guidance brought to your awareness, and when this combines with your strong intuition muscles, a whole world of possibilities opens up to you. It is so much fun!

Learning: Keep Evolving, Growing, and Expanding

This framework has really 10x'ed my life. The universe expands constantly and consistently, and so it goes without saying that we need to grow as well. Tony Robbins said it the best for me: Happiness is the result of people growing and/or contributing. Those two things are the key drivers for any human to feel happy.

In order to focus your learning, it is important to look at the different areas of your life and assess where you are and where you want to go. I have found working with any wheel of life to be very useful. You get to see what is needed to grow that aspect of your life, and your choices become clearer to you. There are many different wheels you can use, but basically you want one which covers all the basic aspects of life. I use the life structures from Michael Beckwith's teachings which include:

- Body Temple or Physical Health
- Spiritual Life
- Ego or Themes where I separate myself from all things love and peace
- Livelihood
- Relationships
- Community or Tribes I engage with
- Beliefs
- Financial Health

As you look at each area, you rate each on a scale of 1 to 10, where 10 is this category at its best and most conscious, and 1 being very low frequency, basically victimhood frequency. With this you are able to see where you would like to grow and/or contribute. Using intuition and manifestations, you could find something new to learn, be inspired to take action around contribution, put in new rituals and routines that take your day to day living to the next level.

Final Words

Improving my intuition has been so important to me. Using mediation to improve my awareness has really leveled up my life. Regular mediation gave me access to a different level of consciousness and opened my mind to what is possible. Try it! You will see the world with a whole new lens.

Your consciousness and awareness will be so much higher that you will be in tune with prompts, those wise whispers, those intuitive flashes, that next best step revealing itself to you. The language you create to have conversations with the universe will take out the noise and help you get to the bottom line quicker. This allows you to take inspired action as you tune in to those relevant insights. The best part is that the more you practice, the better you get at it. Your growth and contribution expands your capacity to receive more clues, insights, and see so much deeper into what could unfold for your best life.

I am living proof that these techniques and practices work! They have taken me from being a trapped, hopeless, powerless child with no way of seeing how life could be better to a now powerful, wise, and happier person who is comfortable with who he is. I am now a powerful manifestor, and I am able to meet the best of life. I truly enjoy moments of love and inner peace.

I would like to leave you with this message: If I can do it, you can too. I started life with everything seemingly stacked against me. I was marginalized early in life and throughout my childhood. I had a lack of trust in the people around me and the world. I had very little knowledge or understanding of anything beyond my limited experience. Yet, I rose above it, and I personally believe that I am stronger because of those obstacles. So as I said, if I can do it, you can too. All you need to do is to start getting quiet and tuning in. Who knows what wonder and magic the world has in store for you!

Education is the most powerful weapon which
you can use to change the world.
~Nelson Mandela (fondly known as Madiba to most South Africans)

About the Author

Brynn is a magical being that is a work of art that is constantly evolving. Based in South Africa, Brynn is a proud gender non-binary being that is part of the LGBT+ community. They have shown through living their life that any marginalized individual (an underdog) can be successful truly being themselves. Brynn works as a Finance Executive for one of the Globe's top management consulting firms and works closely with C-Suite leads looking at transformation at the intersection of technology, business performance, and innovation. Brynn is currently focusing on their passion projects, which address human wellness and helping underdogs (all types of marginalized people) be successful being themselves. They would like to be a sweet inspiration helping people see their power, magic, and to be able to access their power to unlock the best in life for their higher good.

Author Contact Information

Email: Inspire.Empire.77@gmail.com
Instagram: @crazeebe7

Bend it Like Barbie

by Barbie Layton

Passion is a feeling that tells you: this is the right thing to do.
Nothing can stand in my way.
It doesn't matter what anyone else says.
This feeling is so good that it cannot be ignored.
I'm going to follow my bliss and act upon
this glorious sensation of joy.

~Wayne Dyer

Do you remember what you wanted to do when you were a kid? Do you remember the passion that you had for the things that excited you? When I was eight years old I used to dance around in a satin night-gown in my mom's high heels with a baseball bat as a microphone, and I would belt out songs in the living room, thinking that I was performing in front of thousands of people. When you're a kid, you have so many ideas and your imagination is wide open and free. But somehow the world comes in with the 3D reality, and it tells you who it thinks you are. It is absolutely remarkable that we allow ourselves to be conditioned so much by the outside world, and we don't focus on the fact that our own opinion of ourselves is oftentimes the most important, even though other people will tell us what they think that we should be doing.

One of my favorite teachers, Marisa Peer, identifies common phrases like "Who do you think you are?" "You can't do that, you're not that great," "How do you think you're gonna be able to do that?" and "Get real." These are comments that we are all inundated with as we grow up. They become part of our own internal dialogue as we get older.

I just found a ten-page short story that I had written when I was fourteen years old in Honors English class in eighth grade. And on it, I wrote on the cover that I was a world-renowned Best-Selling Author, that I'd been reviewed by the LA Times, The Chicago Tribune, and the New York Times. It sparked a remembrance in me that I had put that into motion forty years ago and lo and behold, that just happened to me that I became an international best-selling author on June 8, 2022, and I was on four New York Times Square billboards! What?? This is bending reality at its finest in reactivating seeds that have been dormant to blossom later in life, and you're never too old to shift your paradigm. Finding that essay reminded me how powerful our words and thoughts are.

When I was a kid, I was exceptionally intelligent. I knew my letter and number blocks at six months, I was reading Dr. Seuss at the age of two, and by the time I got to kindergarten and I was five years old, I already knew how to read chapter books. I had no idea that other kids didn't know how to read. Although it would seem that having these skills was a plus, instead, it put this huge target on my back and started off twelve years of really intense physical and emotional bullying.

Looking back, I also realize that I was like a Young Sheldon of where I didn't get the social cues to understand others. Nobody likes a know-it-all, and that is probably how I came off, but I didn't even realize it. I was just trying to express my natural gifts.

The bullying was intense and included name-calling, spitting in my hair, hurting me on the school bus, pranking me, excluding me, and a lot of things that were really, really painful. It was a clear message to me that I did not belong and that nobody liked me. It became this long cycle of feeling rejected by many groups that set up recurring patterns of experiences later in my life. It was so painful that I can remember these incidents clearly all these years later.

I remember those years as very difficult ones, but with the benefit of hindsight I realized that many of those things were also blessings in disguise. I had to get tough, and thanks to the fact that I had a rebellious streak, I knew that my intelligence and my imagination were things that nobody could ever take away from me. Although I was bullied for these things, I somehow always knew that these were my greatest qualities, and I would not allow others to shake this belief about myself.

My younger years led to some tumultuous teenage years. I, like many of us who grow up with trauma, definitely got up to some no good throughout my teenage years. Having been bullied by people in a small-town environment for more than a decade, I really bought into the belief of the things that people had said about me, and it was incredibly difficult to be able to still continue to try to carve out my own individual identity.

I was often suicidal, depressed, and I turned to very destructive compulsive behaviors that were very unhealthy for me. I realize now that they were coping mechanisms that allowed me to try to see whether or not I could get by and survive in these very difficult circumstances.

When you have an auditorium full of kids that are all screaming at you and you know nobody's going to stop them and no one's going to come to your aid, it's a very terrifying place to be. It's also very isolating and very lonely. I learned not to trust people and I spent a lot of time by myself. I used to play with my dolls a lot and I was a voracious reader, devouring books that allowed me to embody characters in different places and stories, which provided me with an amazing escape.

All of that changed for me when I was in Europe, my junior year of high school when I became an exchange student. I arrived in a very rural tiny village close to the eastern border of Hungary where no one spoke English. I had to figure out very quickly how I was going to be able to survive in that environment. I learned German very quickly, and I was celebrated by all of the different groups that were in different communities. Eureka! It was an epiphany for me to find out that it wasn't me that had been the issue, it was really the small town environment that I had been in, where you never get to evolve or grow.

Unfortunately, there's something called a scapegoat, and most communities have them. A scapegoat is historically somebody that everybody can place all of their anger and their frustration on because it's become sanctioned by a particular group or community that they're allowed to be able to take the brunt of all their criticism. I experienced that when I was a younger child, and you never get a second chance to make a first impression.

Those childhood experiences were tough, but they forced me to be able to focus on my individuality because of the fact that if you don't belong to groups, a lot of times you're also not focusing on the conformity that they are requiring of you. Therefore, you're able to separate and create your own identity. I was into a lot of New Wave and punk rock music in the 1980s, and through a lot of that music, creativity, and crazy fashion coupled with singing and dancing, I was able to really carve out my own true self. It made me feel like I was completely free.

There was a really cool under age club that had a DJ and club lights and I would dance all night, forgetting about any of my troubles. I even earned my own stage spot through my authentic dancing. That was something that made me really happy and brought me a lot of joy.

After college in the 90's, I worked for an auto insurance company that had automated all of their claims to make it where they were taking them via voice rather than in person. I was on a floor of cubicles with over three hundred agents, so I had no idea what their speed was. I got to a point of where I could take a claim in eight minutes and eleven seconds when the average person was taking a claim every hour to an hour and a half. As a result, my superiors posted my name and score and put it in the cubicle of everyone on the floor and notified everybody that I had been able to get to this remarkable eight minute claim procedure.

I thought this would make me well liked, but instead it was like I had a target on my back. Who knew being successful at your job would be threatening to other people? I thought the point of work was to be successful for the company you work for and strive for your personal best. I was asked to be promoted four times over the year, but I could not see a future there, so I was guided to search for something new. I ended up finding a job teaching English to students in South Korea, in the 90's, before Korea was modernized.

From there, I ended up in a regular job working for over 25 years. I found myself back in a situation that oftentimes replicated that same situation that I experienced when I was a child. This is a common occurrence with people. They find themselves back in the same situation over and over, especially when it was something like this, a childhood wound that some refer to as a core wound. From that core wound you then replicate other relationships around your life that are the same as the one you experienced as a child, and you also look for evidence and proof that the things people told you about yourself were true. This is usually an unconscious behavior.

My core wound was being rejected as a child. It was not surprising that I ended up in a position where I was again rejected by my coworkers. I was recreating my core wounding.

Luckily, I was good at my job. I was focusing exclusively on my clients and the very best for them, and I was having really remarkable results. I even had a consultant fly from New York to document my techniques, but my coworkers were not happy about that because I upset the status quo, and I wasn't just conforming and doing what everybody else was doing. To me, the success of my clients was more important than the acceptance of my coworkers, but my coworkers and superiors were cruel in putting me in my place whenever they could.

There have been sociological studies done in the 20th century where they showed that people that were working for a phone answering company, when somebody pushed forward and was able to surpass what the status quo or the average was, that they generally would ostracize or make that person feel bad or get them to quit, because everybody wanted to be able to stay in the status quo, because that meant they didn't have to work harder. Other people don't like to see that, and it makes them feel somehow that you're trying to show them up or that you're trying to be better than them, even though you're just trying to do a good job and strive for personal excellence.

In my life, I've experienced three near death experiences, and I've had a lot of trauma in my life. But in 2016, I was officially diagnosed with a chronic immunosuppressive disease that is not curable. My life had been so full with travel and doing things all over the world that it shrunk my life to the point where I could only focus on going to work, going home, and putting an ice pack on my stomach to be able to take care of the pain while feeling fatigued. I didn't have the energy or the ability to do a lot of the social activities I had done before.

To me, it was my own personal pandemic, and I felt like something needed to shift. I suffered for three years with this excruciating pain and having absolutely no support at work, with a boss who had absolutely no sympathy for me and coworkers who had no compassion for the fact that I was suffering since I didn't "look" sick. I had to go to battle multiple times to defend myself.

In 2019, I heard about a personal development course which looked at every area of your life. I decided to do the course because it was a time when I knew that I knew I had to change my life. I just sat there and I prayed and I said, "Please, something has to shift. I cannot live this life like this any longer. I'm isolated and alone and focusing exclusively on just existing."

I have always had a service mindset, and I was still achieving at such a high level with my clientele, however, at the same time, I was personally suffering. I had hoped that this new program would help me figure out what I needed to do to change my life. The program was amazing, it helped me to examine all areas of my life and decide what I wanted in each area. It really gave me that opportunity to search deeply into each area of my life and see that although there were many things on the outside that looked like success, on the inside, I was still so unfulfilled and so detached from anything feeling like it was a good thing. The program helped me clarify my desires and goals. I now knew what I wanted, but I didn't know how I could get from where I was to where I wanted to go.

That was when I discovered that you could actually rewire your brain. I found two teachers, Marisa Peer and Christie Marie Sheldon, who really resonated with me. They were talking about unlimited abundance and shifting your mindset so you could begin to attract the things you want towards you. I dove deep into their work.

I began attending events for personal transformation and they were amazing. Being surrounded by like minded people inspired me and learning from world class teachers was amazing. I learned from a lot of great teachers at these events, and I felt so excited by the possibilities. One of the events I went to was called Mindvalley Live, and I was able to meet the owner of the company, Vishen Lakhiani, as well as some amazing teachers like Keith Ferrazzi and Lisa Nichols. It was an incredible experience.

Right after that event, the Coronavirus pandemic came in 2020 and the entire world shut down. At that moment, I knew for a fact that I had a choice. I was either going to feel sorry for myself and go into panic mode like a lot of people were and feel like this was the end of the world, or I was going to throw myself into everything I possibly could with going into the personal transformational principles.

I decided to dive into transformation. I have been on a Facebook group with Vishen and other people since 2019 which helped me to expand my beliefs. The "Buddha and the Badass" came out and then he moved everything onto the Zoom platforms, where we were really blessed to be able to have the Mindvalley university that went live in August 2020. Naveen Jain came out and said the most amazing things about, "What are you willing to die for? What are you willing to be able to focus on to be able to make your life better so that you're not sleepwalking through your life?"

I realized at that moment that I really needed to start focusing back on the mission that I had when I was a kid. That was performing, singing, dancing, speaking, serving, and writing. I had put all of that on the back burner because many of us believe that after a certain age our life is static, and then it's already been determined for us. We just continue through that course and just continue doing the same thing no matter what, because we feel like we've already been aligned to it. But things are shiftable, changeable, malleable. We can change our brains, which is called neuroplasticity, and I was able to do this. I rewired my brain and this changed everything for me. My mission is to show others that if I can do it, you can do it!

I completed every course available and I began seeing results. I had manifested more abundance than I ever had. I learned so much and I was changing fast. I was lucky that I had found online communities that supported me during this time. We all learned and grew together.

I joined the premium coaching program that Vishen Lakhiani offered through his online educational platform, Mindvalley. It was an incredible opportunity to be mentored by Vishen himself. There were only 30 people in the group, and it was amazing. I even manifested the funds to pay for it! It became a gamification extraordinaire! That's where I met Kerry Fisher in October of 2020, and other amazing entrepreneurs that have become lifelong friends. All of us really started focusing on the Mindvalley principles in the sense of becoming the best 3d version of ourselves within the 5D reality. We were working off of no limits and supporting each other in our journeys! I started doing professional intuitive consulting sessions with people and having absolutely amazing results.

I had the opportunity to be on The Best You Expo virtually, from the side stage in August 2020 to the main stage with Ken Honda and Lisa Nichols in January of 2021. Things just kept getting better and better and the trajectory was like a supernova. Then, I landed my own TV channel on The Best You TV! Quelle surprise! My first two guests were Naveen Jain and Ken Honda, which was surreal! I've since had 40 world thought leaders that I've interviewed about beautiful things in regards to making the world a better place and starting the kindness revolution. All of this was beyond my wildest dreams, but I was living the Mindvalley principles! It was incredible that all the things I had dreamed of, all the things I had thought about as I did the Lifebook course, were coming true.

The main thing I wanted to convey through my story was that each one of us has the ability to create the life we want to create.

How Do You Create a Total Life Transformation?

Ultimately, many of those things with making a life change is that you have to be able to reshift yourself into looking at where you are in the moment. I focused on extreme gratitude and being able to be grateful for all of the physical things that are supporting you; like your bed, your stove, your refrigerator, your shower, your toilet, your computer, the internet service, the people at the water company, it was literally a blessing back and forth. Then I started to thank the people that had been able to bring food to my door, and when we look at all of these supports that we take for granted that are there in our infrastructure, we can then start to focus on re-shifting our entire mindset.

That's what I love about Mindvalley, the focusing on the abundance mindset in all facets of your life; body, mind, spirit. I loved all of that information. Being able to say yes to the universe means re-falling in love with yourself. Finding a way to see what's good about you as opposed to focusing on the flaws. And then from there, reigniting the dreams that you thought that had died within you. Then, finally, becoming the VIP of your own life. When you do those three things, when you reignite those things, you reinvigorate your life. This adds extra energy and frequency to that which we had basically allowed to go dormant.

By having that opportunity to be able to do that, I opened myself up to multiple communities all over the world. Every time I would say yes to the universe, I would open myself up to those different communities. Once I got invited in, I realized that I already knew 20 to 30% of the people that were already there.

I have built some absolutely amazingly beautiful friendships, built businesses, and I was just in *Women Gone Wild,* a wealth edition book to empower women to step into their authentic voices that became an international bestseller on June 8, 2022, and is now in 46 countries and 18 languages. The trajectory of everything that has happened is due to the fact that you have to suspend disbelief and you have to stay in a state of childlike wonder, and having that sense of being an adult doesn't have to be so serious. And really, even though we're looking at real things in real time, it's also important to go back and heal the old traumas and issues that we had earlier in life, so that we can step into the greatest version of ourselves that we possibly can.

I'm absolutely and positively still a work in progress. I still have a lot of growing and healing to do. But by being able to say yes to the universe, I magnetized a documentary that I filmed with Dr. John Demartini in

Houston in May that will be coming out in 2023. And I will be in an additional book series as well.

I have been lucky to help build with people who are like minded that I call heart centered conscious entrepreneurs. I am in a Mastermind group with Denis Waitley himself, and I am writing for the Los Angeles Tribune. These are all amazing opportunities that I would have once thought were not ever available to me, but they are all coming my way now that I have done all this work on myself. I know other opportunities that seem almost impossible, but they become these golden opportunities that come out of nowhere because I was bold enough to step into that bending reality space. It is in that space that you realize you can create anything and that you need to simply focus on the fact that thoughts are things. First we think about it, then we can achieve it.

The friendships that I've developed with people that have come forward and all these beautiful spaces is a testament to the fact that when we open ourselves up to new frequencies and new opportunities, our worlds can change very dramatically.

Right now, I'm in a state of perturbation, and that means that I'm still in the old paradigm while I'm stepping into the new paradigm. But all of this is literally almost like the chrysalis of the butterfly having an opportunity to be able to metamorphosize into something completely different from what you were before. No longer the caterpillar, but allowing yourself to become a butterfly.

Again, your opinion of yourself is the most important thing that matters. Not everyone is going to understand your vision. Not everyone's going to be able to relate to what you're accomplishing and what you're doing. Unfortunately, people do get jealous and they get competitive. That is human nature, and ultimately that has to be part of the process. Being able to intentionally step into these beautiful spaces, to be of service to humanity is the thing to focus on. When you are in that state, you can't lose because when you are focusing on something bigger than yourself, you can achieve anything. It's not about the money, it's not about the ego, it's not about the success. It's about connection.

So go out and find the community that works for you. Community is literally the most important thing for us as humans, and we are suffering from not being connected and being so isolated from each other.

If you have taken this last couple of years to be able to be introspective, and to evaluate yourself in an honest fashion, then you can also have the opportunity to become the best version of yourself, and you can have the opportunity to become a hero. A hero, to me, is someone who inspires others by example to show that it is never too late to change directions of your life, and to step back into the authenticity of your purpose to reconnect to the seeds of who you wanted to be when you were little and realigning into your purpose and joy.

About the Author

Barbie Layton is an international best-selling author, speaker, performer, and intuitive healer and consultant that works with CEO's and individuals to re-fall in love with themselves, re-animate their dreams, and become the VIP of their own lives. She is a California native and has lived on three continents, visited over 35 countries and all United States. She is a global citizen that works with different communities and has worked with Holocaust survivors, Vietnamese and Cambodian refugees, and other populations that have allowed her to be of service. She now works as a leader of leaders to help shift organizations to optimize their harmony and increase their monetization. She is also a television host on The Best You TV, where she interviews world thought leaders and an active member in the MindValley community. She has also been featured in over fifty podcasts internationally.

Author Contact Information

Email: intuitivebarbie1@gmail.com
Website: www.barbielayton.com

Everyone thinks of changing the world,
but no one thinks of changing himself.

~Leo Tolstoy

It's Time to Make a Change

by Eva Marková

I thought other people could make me happy.
I didn't look for happiness within.
I was trying to love and please everybody except myself.
Today I have a new approach.
I put myself first and I attract people into my life
who love and respect me naturally.

~Eva Marková

F or a very long time, I felt lost in life. I didn't know where I was going, I had no true direction. I embarked on many adventures, traveled the world, and had lots of fun. I often felt that I was getting close to what I wanted, but each time, something would happen and before I knew it, I would be right back where I started. I repeated this pattern so many times. It was exhausting. I kept trying, but eventually the search left me feeling completely overwhelmed. I felt like I had fallen to my knees and I wasn't sure how I was going to pull myself back up. I had lost my zest for life. It was a scary time for me, because I had never felt anything like this before. I realized I was doing something wrong, and that I had to start looking for new ways to live my life.

During this period, I turned inward. I thought about my life, searching for answers. I thought about my childhood and how I had always done everything I was told to do, I had always tried to be perfect. I went through primary school with all A's, and then I studied economics. Ultimately, I graduated with great success and immediately went to work, holding down a great job. I had done everything I was supposed to do, which was why I was so shocked that I was struggling so much. I kept thinking, "I'm the girl with the straight A's at school, the girl who always handled everything well, the girl who went out and got a great job, I had it all!" So why was I sitting here feeling like I couldn't breathe?

I had all the success I could imagine in life, yet I still wasn't happy. I had zero confidence in myself. I knew I had to do something about it. I realized that school taught me how to memorize things and put them down on the paper at the time of an exam. But school had never taught me the things I needed to do to really flourish in life. I had never been taught to look after myself. I had never been taught to love myself. Instead, I had only heard criticism, judgment, and negativity my whole life from every authority figure around me.

I started to wonder if I was the only person who thought that this is not the way to live a life. I began to ask my friends and family how they felt, and I was shocked because it seemed as if everyone just accepted that this is all life could be. I tried to explain how I felt to people, but it seemed as if nobody really listened to what I had to say. They simply didn't understand me, and I felt that nobody took me seriously. After all, I was just a nineteen year old girl, what could I possibly know? I began to think that maybe I needed to be like everyone else. Maybe I should get a boyfriend and an apartment and settle down like all the other girls were doing. Maybe that was the answer. But then I thought about my last relationship and how I ultimately had to leave because of my boyfriend's never ending complaining and negativity. I wasn't sure a relationship was the right way to go. I was lost.

That was when I decided I had to do something. I decided I should go to Spain. I had heard a lot about Spain and thought I would like it there. Plus, I realized it was easy to get there from where I lived in the Czech Republic. All I had to do was take a bus to get there. I began to ask friends if they were interested in joining me. I asked around for a few months, but nobody was willing to leave their familiar lives. I wasn't sure I wanted to go alone, so I kept asking people if they wanted to travel with me.

One day, I bumped into an acquaintance. It was a guy that I didn't know very well but as we were talking, he told me he was planning to go to the United States. He asked me if I wanted to go with him. I wasn't sure. After all, the United States was super far away, all the way across the ocean. I wasn't sure I was brave enough to venture so far from my homeland. Although part of me yearned for adventure, another part wasn't so sure I could possibly go so far away. Could I really fly all the way across the world and start a new life there?

A part of me really wanted to go but another part, the fearful part, doubted I could. I kept thinking, "Can I really do this? How will I find a job? Am I good enough?" As I thought about it, I realized that I simply didn't have the confidence, I didn't think I was good enough for life like that. And then I realized, "Oh, no, I'm thinking the same way as the people around me. I'm thinking I am not enough." I continued to think about it and uncovered a lot of feelings related to my belief that I was simply not enough. Not smart enough, not brave enough, not good enough.

But then I thought, "Am I really not good enough?" I wasn't sure, I felt insecure. I truly didn't know the answer. I reflected upon the fact that all my life I had heard the same thing. That I wasn't good enough, that I couldn't do it. I had heard it so much that I had started to believe it myself. I was at a turning point. I knew that it was time for me to make a change, and I was so eager for a change. I was just so unsure, so afraid of everything. Yet, deep inside, I knew that only I could create the life I wanted. If I wanted change, I was the one who had to take action.

Things began to happen very fast. After all, when you set events into action, they sometimes take on a life of their own. That's what happened for me and before I knew it, my friend and I were sending in our visa applications together. Then we were on the way to the US embassy in Prague, the capital of the Czech Republic. We had to go for an interview with the immigration officer so that he could decide if we were eligible or not. I was so nervous. But I kept remembering that I was embracing change. I could do this.

As we went to the next line, we thought we were getting an interview but tto my surprise, instead of an interview, there was just a line of applicants waiting. When it was my turn, the officer stamped our passports with a "Declined" stamp and threw them back at us with a loud "NEXT". Oh my! I was in shock. That "I'm not good enough" sentence kept playing in my head like a broken record. I was crushed.

My friend was not one to give up, though. While we were in Prague, close to the travel agency, we decided we needed to make a decision. We had to make a plan for what we would do next. We decided a one way ticket to Thailand was the best option. We figured we could make our way through South East Asia and then see where the wind blows. We would go to Thailand and then eventually either fly back home or continue on to Australia or New Zealand. We had a plan and it was even bigger than the US trip. I was excited and nervous, but committed to this.

As we made our way back to our town, the broken record about not being good enough continued to play in my mind. I was so worried about telling my parents about what I was planning to do. I knew they would not be happy, but I wanted this change. I knew I had no choice, and I had to tell them. I strengthened my resolve to go regardless of how my parents felt. I was taking my life into my own hands, I was creating the life I desired and I understood that this was the natural course of events. My parents were nervous at first, but they were supportive and before I knew it, it was time to travel.

The trip was incredible. We traveled to Thailand, Malaysia, Singapore, and Indonesia, and it was more than I could ever have imagined. Eventually, my friend decided to go back home, and we said goodbye in Jakarta. I wanted to continue my adventures, so I decided to fly to New Zealand by myself. I marveled at my bravery. In a few short months, I had completely transformed. The energy and good vibes from the people I met along the way allowed me to see there was a different world out there than I was used to. Traveling was my very first taste of freedom, and I loved it. I wanted more.

Although my confidence was rising, I still had some of the old fears within me. After all, I was a young woman, all alone. I had very little money, as a matter of fact, after I paid for my flight to New Zealand, I had only about $300 US dollars to my name. I also wasn't fluent in English, even though I had taken four years of English in school. Plus, I had no job and no idea how to find one once I got to New Zealand. These thoughts were like a broken record, swirling around in my head, threatening to overwhelm me.

Then the guilt came in. I thought about my family, and how the only connection I had with them in the last three months was a few postcards and one letter I sent to them. We didn't have mobile phones or any devices, and back then the internet was limited. When I traveled, I was truly isolated, all alone, I knew there would be nobody else but me to depend on. I looked deep within and found that I still had those thoughts that I wasn't good enough. I had heard that my entire life from everyone around me, but now here I was telling myself that I wasn't good enough. I had let the message sink in so deep that I now actually believed it. I did it so automatically that I didn't even know why. I reached within and found the strength. I *was* good enough, I *could* do this. I was going.

When I finally arrived in New Zealand, I was amazed by the beauty of the country. And the people! I couldn't believe how kind and welcoming they were. I had been completely blown away by the kindness of the people I had met in South East Asia but in New Zealand, it was next level. It was like kindness on steroids. I felt so welcomed and finally, for the first time in my life, I felt like I belonged. I was finally discovering who I really was. Or perhaps, I was simply remembering who I was underneath all the conditioning. I felt free.

I met many amazing travelers and locals during my time in New Zealand. I only had a year there, so I decided to take short term jobs so I could have the flexibility to experience every corner of the country. I worked my way around the country, taking short term jobs so that I could easily see every corner of the country. It was a blissful time for me.

One day, I was reflecting on my grand adventure and I realized that the record in my mind had changed from "I am not enough," to "Life is great! I am great! I made it!"

I was so thrilled as I thought about all I had accomplished. Here I was, in a tiny country on the other side of the world, away from everyone and everything I knew, and I was having the time of my life. I didn't have much contact with the people back home, after all, we didn't have cell phones back then, but every once in a while I would buy a phone card and I would be able to call my family from a public phone booth. When I called them, I was so surprised by how supportive they had become. I wondered if they had changed their mind about me. Had they realized that I was not that useless after all? I played with this thought after every call I made to my family and it made me really happy.

In my mind, I imagined what would happen when I finally returned home. I thought everything would change. That there would be no more negativity, nobody criticizing me anymore. I figured life would be as amazing once I got home as it was here. I was happy.

After twelve months in New Zealand, I decided to head back to Europe. I was super excited to see my family. I was totally convinced that my family's attitude towards me had changed. I thought that life would be different. Unfortunately, it wasn't that way. The first disappointment came right after I landed in Prague. I got off the plane and went into the terminal and I realized that people were not smiling. What happened? And then I remembered that this was the way it was here. I had completely forgotten about this attitude during the fifteen months I was away.

I was disappointed, but then remembered all the calls with my family when I was in New Zealand. I figured that as long as my family's attitude had changed, I would be fine. And it was fine for the first few days home but then, as soon as the excitement of the lost daughter returning home evaporated, everything went back to the same old criticism and negativity. Slowly but surely, as the time passed, my broken record about not being good enough sneaked back into my mind.

A few months after I returned to the Czech Republic, I found a job at a nearby office. One day, while I was at work, I was at my desk listening to everyone talking around me. All I heard was complaining, yelling, blaming, arguing, and bickering. My head began to spin and I felt terrible.

I closed my eyes and brought myself back to New Zealand. I imagined the pristine nature and the kind, joyous people. As my imagination took me back, I could smell the ocean and the flowers of a Pohutukawa tree. It felt like home. I relaxed. Then I opened my eyes and fell back into reality.

I was back in the Czech Republic, in an office building surrounded by miserable people. I felt like I couldn't breathe, like I was going to suffocate here. And right then and there, I made a decision to leave. I was going back to New Zealand! Decision made.

I ended up going back to New Zealand, and it has now been thirteen years since I first landed there. There have been some ups and downs in my new homeland, but I am happy. I spent many years taking temporary jobs in New Zealand so that I would have the freedom to travel the world, and that has been incredible. The things I have seen and heard, the sights and sounds of all the different countries I have been to have opened my mind and nourished my soul. I mostly travel solo, which helped me to mix in with the locals in every country I have visited. These experiences have changed me a lot. I know that for sure.

These travels have allowed me to build my confidence, but I am still a work in progress. Although I feel stronger and quite capable, there are still times that I allow other people to take away my feelings of strength and confidence. I am a people pleaser, and I have a hard time saying no to people. I really care what people say about me and think about me, so I am working on that.

A couple of years ago, I moved to a bigger city for a better job. I decided it was time to settle down and have a more stable, full time job. I lived with my boyfriend, a Pacific Islander born in Auckland. Although there are many red flags in our relationship, I ignore them all. For some strange reason I tend to ignore when people treat me with disrespect, and that includes my boyfriend. I am in love with my boyfriend, so I am willing to put up with a lot.

My boyfriend asked me to marry him and I agreed, in spite of all the red flags. After all, isn't this what we are supposed to do? You meet someone; you get married, get a mortgage, and have kids, that's life. That's what people in my community do, and there is still a part of me that wants to be like them. I don't want to feel like I'm different. I simply ignore the red flags, I close my eyes and pretend they don't exist. We got married, and just after our wedding we decided to move to Australia. My boyfriend moved first, finding an apartment in Perth while I finalized everything in New Zealand. During this time, I began to have a very uneasy feeling like something was very wrong. I ignored the feeling, and continued to wrap up everything I needed to in New Zealand, before getting on the plane to Perth to join my husband.

I was very excited to begin my new life, and couldn't wait to get to our apartment complex. I had already met the neighbors and we had bonded immediately. I couldn't wait to get to know them better. When I got to my apartment complex, though, I was immediately aware that something was off. All of my neighbors, who had always been so friendly and talkative, were acting strangely. They would look away from me and quickly disappear into their own apartments. It was so strange. Before long, I realized that my worst nightmare had come true. My husband was seeing somebody else.

The next months were terrible. I felt immense stress as I sat there, in the middle of this conflict, listening to all the lies and stories he was telling me. I began to feel a constant pain in my chest. I couldn't sleep, I couldn't eat, I couldn't think. Our marriage lasted only six months.

I decided to fly back to New Zealand. I wanted to be surrounded by friends who loved me. I was not ashamed to tell them what happened and I got plenty of support from my friends. It helped me to get through the pain and grief to be able to speak so freely about what had happened and how I felt. I hadn't expected this type of support, but I welcomed it. This was another dark time for me. At times I drank alcohol to numb the pain, at other times I sat and cried. I experienced huge mood swings. One moment I was happy, thinking how lucky I was that this unhealthy relationship ended sooner rather than later, and the next moment I was ready to pick up the phone and try to save my marriage. I felt like a crazy person.

During this time, I was struggling greatly. I had trouble sleeping, often only falling asleep in the early morning hours. There were days I couldn't get out of bed in the morning. Most of the time I was late to work, and my coworkers encouraged me to seek help. They said that I was depressed and that I needed medication. That frightened me, because although part of me thought I was depressed, the word medication scared me. I didn't want to take drugs to fix this. I had to find a better solution.

I took a close look at my life. Although I was happy to be back in New Zealand, I was living in the same house and driving the same car that I used to share with my ex-husband. I was working at the same job that we both used to work at, and it wasn't even a great job because I was on a fixed weekly salary. Each month, when I paid for all my expenses, I had nothing left over. I felt like I was back where I had started so many years before. The little self-esteem and confidence I had gained over the last decade had gone down the drain.

I wondered what I was going to do with my life and what I should do next. Once again, I found myself lost and unsure. Then, an idea came to me. I thought I would use the last of my savings and go to Tahiti and the surrounding French Polynesian Islands. I knew it was a crazy idea, but travel had always been the way forward for me, so I decided to take the leap of faith and booked a flight. I immediately felt better. I realized that the magic of making a change was making all the difference. Sitting at home and feeling sorry for myself didn't work, but this new adventure certainly had changed my outlook.

I planned the trip as I went along. I would fly from one tiny island to another, picking them as I went. I met some amazing people on the way and did some exciting new things, like completing my scuba diving course in the most amazing locations I could ever dream of. It was an incredibly healing time for me, especially because I had lots of time to reflect on what had happened. I allowed myself to process all of it and slowly but surely, I felt better. Eventually, I decided to move back home to my family in the Czech Republic. And there I was, back where I grew up, back where I started.

Still broken-hearted yet excited to restart my life in my hometown, I got a new job and a new boyfriend. It was a new life, a new routine. The job was fine, except for the office politics. Arguing, blaming, and gossiping happened on a daily basis. I felt unsafe, like I had to watch my back at all times. My boyfriend was very nice, but he definitely liked me to do things his way. If I wanted to have a say at something important it immediately started a fight. I realized that I was truly back to where I started. Back to the traditional life I had run from so many years before. I realized that my boyfriend had the same mindset as my parents and the people I grew up with. He was quick to blame and point the finger if anything went wrong, but he never wanted to discuss anything. It was exactly the opposite of the life I had been leading for the past fifteen years when I traveled the world, exactly the opposite of the life I wanted.

For some time, I did my best to ignore all these negativities, but before long I found myself slowly giving in and slowly becoming like everyone around me. I would catch myself complaining about everything and everyone, blaming other people and having negative thoughts all the time. My confidence was at an all time low. It felt like it was back down to zero. I wondered, is it time to make a change again? And if so, what should I change this time?

Although my years of travel had been amazing, I realized that moving from one side of the world to the other simply does not work! I knew I needed help, but who was going to help me? Who was willing to help me? I felt like everybody in my life put me on the bottom of their list. I felt like nobody believed in me and I didn't matter at all. It was affecting all aspects of my life. I was tired all the time. I couldn't get to sleep at night and I was having trouble waking up in the mornings to go to work. My body hurt, I felt pains in different parts of my body for no reason I could determine.

I was feeling so down that I turned to food. I would eat to make myself feel better, but that only helps for a little while. Then I would have to eat more to fill up the emptiness I felt inside. It didn't help. The only outcome of this was gaining weight, but I continued to do it anyway.

I found myself playing the movie of my life in my mind all the time. I would go over what I had done, where I had been, I was trying to find out who I was. As I replayed my life in my mind, I found myself blaming myself for everything. Every single mistake I had made ran through my head. I blamed myself for my broken marriage and felt it was my fault that I was divorced. I blamed myself for not being able to fit in where I lived now and as I thought about it, it seemed that I had felt that way for a lot of my life.

I began to live in the past, thinking about all the good times I had while traveling the world. I realized that I was really depressed, and considered if I needed medication. I was in a dark place, and I simply could not see the light at the end of the tunnel.

Christmas was approaching. I had no energy at all at the end of another endless work day. I sat in front of my computer, browsing the internet. Suddenly an advertisement for an online course came up on my computer screen. For some reason, the woman speaking immediately caught my attention. She was a world class therapist, and I was absolutely amazed by her words. I resonated with so much of what she was saying.

I decided to buy the course and spent every day of my Christmas break watching it. It utterly changed my life. She was talking about mindset and discussed how important it was to pay attention to the way we talk to ourselves. She also said that we are ruled by our thoughts, so we should be careful of the thoughts we allow in our heads. I realized that although I was depressed, perhaps I didn't need medication after all. I was eager to try her technique.

I began to pay attention to the thoughts in my head and the way that I talked to myself. I began to notice that I had a lot of "limiting beliefs" which were holding me back. I realized that so many of my thoughts were centered on what I had done wrong, the mistakes I had made, how I was not good enough in so many areas. Once I began to truly pay attention to my mind, I couldn't believe the type of thoughts that raced through my mind nonstop.

This began a period of intense self examination. I get deep into analyzing my thoughts, my self-talk, and my unhealthy patterns throughout my life. I notice that things are starting to change, I am starting to change. The way I look at myself starts to change as well. I finally understand how important it is to love and look after myself. I feel an urge rising in me to simply scream to the whole world: "Look, here I am, and I do matter!"

These changes in me and in my life inspire me to search for more personal growth teachers. I learned to meditate daily and visualize my future life. This seems so simple, but the practice allowed me to feel calm and grounded. I now sleep better and have more energy during the day. Visualizing my future allows me to begin to set goals for bringing that future into reality. I looked at every area of my life and envisioned what I wanted in that area. I write about my vision and read through it often to remind myself of it. I learn not to worry about how I will get there, I just hold my vision in my mind.

Amazingly, I noticed that many new opportunities came my way. Having a clear vision of what I wanted was a big missing piece in my life, and creating the vision allowed many things to fall into place without too much effort. In the past, I had tried to simply push through everything without any real idea of where I wanted to go. This led to very few results. With my new power of visualization, I notice immediate results. It seems that just by being clear about what I want, I am able to attract a lot into my life very effortlessly.

I also started a daily gratitude practice. Every night I go to sleep thinking about things I'm grateful for and each morning, before I get up, I think about these things. Even on days when nothing major happened, I realized that there are so many small wins to be grateful for. As I continued my gratitude practice I noticed that some days I would get a rush of gratitude during the day for no reason, which is a truly amazing feeling. This is a very powerful practice that brought lots of abundance into many areas of my life.

I also got to work changing my beliefs. One very important belief that I changed was that I was not worthy, that somehow, I was not enough. I changed that belief and replaced it with the belief that I am enough, and I do deserve the things that I desire. This was a true game changer for me because now, when I want to have something in my life, I truly believe I deserve to have it. I don't have any doubts at the back of my mind any more. My broken record of not being good enough had left my mind for good.

Most importantly, I learned how to love myself and put myself first. And no, it is not selfish to do that. Only when I am strong and well can I do my best for others around me. In the old days, I used to put everybody else first. I was weak, and I was also an easy target for those who just wanted to use me. That no longer happens. Today, I feel strong in my decisions and opinions, and I do not worry about what people say or think about me.

As I began to heal and change my beliefs about myself, my relationships improved as well. The relationship with my parents improved a lot. This happened because I was learning a lot about forgiveness, which allowed me to come to an understanding that my parents had done their best with the knowledge they had at the time. Forgiving my parents allowed me to forgive others as well. Best of all, it allowed me to forgive myself for all my past mistakes, my missteps, and what I used to perceive as my flaws. Now, I realized that I had also always done my best with the knowledge I had with the time. This set me free. Since I began to love myself and I was able to set boundaries, my relationships improved dramatically.

I came to understand that everything is up to me. I was the one who had the ability to do things differently. Now it is up to me to do things differently. And I will.

I can see myself as a completely different person now. For the first time in my life I feel like I'm going to be ok. I don't live in the past, and I also don't worry about my future as I did before. I live right here, right now. I'm happy with what I have in my life, and I know that when I want more I have the strength, the courage, and most importantly, the right mindset to go and get it.

I feel like I've just crossed the starting line of my transformation journey. I can see many changes in my life; changes I would never believe were possible for me. I am proud of myself for that, but there is still a lot more to explore, and I can't wait to see what the future has in store for me. Instead of fearing the future, I am excited about it.

Today, I am proud to say that I am not the girl with straight A's at school who lacks confidence any more. I am the girl with straight A's in life who has entered a new path of education. I am on the path to living the life I know I was meant to live. The life of fun, excitement, and joy that I know I deserve.

When you don't feel satisfied in life,
do not just wait for something to happen,
embrace a change.
~Eva Marková

About the Author

Eva Markova was born and raised in a small village in Czechoslovakia, now called the Czech Republic. She has an education in economics and accounting. Instead of building a career in her major she decided to leave her home country at a very young age and travel the world. At the age of twenty, she left the country on a one way ticket to Thailand. After traveling throughout Asia, she moved to New Zealand, where she lived for fifteen years before moving back to the Czech Republic in 2015. Travelling is still her biggest passion.

At the age of forty, Eva discovered the magic of personal growth, and it led her down a new entrepreneurial path. She built a network of fun, authentic, caring, and ambitious people who are not afraid to dream big. She became an investor and is involved in several trading projects, which gives her more freedom than she ever had as an employee.

Eva considers her family to be most important to her. She loves spending time in nature and still travels the world, seeking fun and adventure as she goes. Her mission is to share her knowledge and her life experience to help people achieve freedom and to encourage them to lead an amazing lifestyle.

Author Contact Information

Email: yestoabundantlife@gmail.com
Website: yestoabundantlife.com

The Living in Alignment Approach

by Shyla Melwani

*Choosing your alignment is one of your
greatest gifts to the planet. Period.*

~Peta Kelly

open by sharing my story with you. The start of this decade marked an insane year for the world. This challenge changed all our lives. The change in this new world put me in an awkward phase where my old self was gone, but my new self wasn't fully born yet.

It didn't help that while going through troubles, my best friend ever so casually told me, "Shyla, you're getting fat and lazy." Wow – that one hit me hard. I remember feeling my throat close, and my eyes swell up. I became motionless on the outside but began to choke on the inside. I was shocked at the comment – not because what he said was wrong, but because he was right!

I felt that comment's heartache hit me deeply, like a ton of bricks was thrown directly into my heart. I was already feeling lethargic, depressed, lost and directionless; needless to say, this comment left me feeling disheveled – because he was right. Physically, I had let myself go, gaining over 30kg quickly. Mentally, I was undergoing a challenging transformation from the weight and other problems that an unhappy mind attracts. I was hurting, and I was in deep, physical pain.

My mother always told me that from a higher perspective, being challenged is good, as it requires you to go inward to find the answers you seek. During this trying time, my mother's words kept ringing, "Where there is a challenge is precisely where growth lies."

And so, I decided to prove to my friend – nay, not to him – I decided to prove MYSELF wrong. I decided to change this pain into power. I decided that would be the last day someone openly called me 'fat' and 'lazy'. I decided my solution would be to align my energies with the NEW person I wanted to become.

After finally realizing that aligning my human self with my spiritual or energetic self brings immense benefits and a new life (no exceptions), I began focusing my energies on the brilliant internal practice of Living in Alignment. Aligning myself with the new state of being I craved helped me become one with my desires. Daily alignment became a part of my well-being, and the benefits it brought me were numerous and fulfilling: I began respecting myself, which allowed me to befriend myself and finally enjoy spending alone time with just me and my thoughts for hours on end.

This led me to become self-empowered and spend much time in my own world, using the precious time to get creative and ask how to serve the world more through my books and podcasts. I embodied a new persona of total self-confidence, self-worth, and self-appreciation. I expanded and reprogrammed my mind and belief systems. Best of all, I learnt how to stay present by living the perspective that life is just a test of how present you can be – this mind-blowing thought transformed my spiritual and energetic playing field – not only was I in the arena now, but I was playing my best game as a human being.

The Process

I began the search for an inner guide – an inward self-help tool – to help me get through this inner battle, because all great things begin from the inside. I understood that to change the physical body, the insides must first change. These 'insides' are:

- your choice of thoughts
- your choice of self-talk
- your choice of words
- your choice of action

Yes, everything is a choice, and when you choose to change these (because you can!), your mind attracts these new thoughts and words like an energetic magnet, and everything outside of you (your physical reality) begins to change!

Learning that the mind is carefully planned and meticulously designed in this magnetic (energetic) way for your own benefit helps you to understand that you can attract whatever you are in harmonious vibration with (like attracts like); this knowledge helps you play the game of energy, USE vibration to your complete advantage, and HAVE fun living an exciting life!

I vibrationally braced myself for what this energetic act of aligning my thoughts, words, and actions would bring me. It was time for my rebirth, and boy, did the universe deliver me a brand new slate.

The process of aligning myself vibrationally to the physical body I sought for, as well as the mental clarity I yearned for, called me to learn that working on my alignment is an emotional journey and anything emotional is ENERGETIC (e-motion = energy in motion). Nothing is worth investing thought into without an emotional stake in it, anyway. Tending to the emotional (energetic) journey cleverly gives you precisely what you want. When you tend to the emotional (energetic) journey of alignment, this universe has the resources and the cleverness to orchestrate for the person what you want—it is great fun to watch and be a part of!

So, I began the process of Living in Alignment, and a new world opened up.

Be Proactive

In this chapter, I shared with you the Living in Alignment approaches that I used to feel nourished, fulfilled, and thriving in my times of hardship. This chapter is proactive; it requires deliberate action and effort for what you want to come to fruition.

Because these daily actions saved and completely transformed my life, I suggest you study it to benefit from it and try to understand that you will attract whatever you are in harmonious vibration with. I have intentionally included reasonable and logical practices on what to do and HOW to do it because of my sincere desire to be helpful to you. However, remember 'the thing' about self-help—all the advice in the world will not help you until you are ready to help yourself.

At the end of the chapter, I provide questions to call yourself out on and call-to-actions that I encourage you not just to answer in your mind but write down on paper, because there is pure magic and transformative power in putting pen to paper. You always need to find out where the written word can take you – and it is an exciting thought that you can be led there simply through your handwriting. Your word is your wand.

The Key

By far, the KEY to unlocking this new version of myself – an expression of the new me, my new state of being – a masterpiece of myself, is ALIGNMENT. I aligned myself by being an aligned person – that is, a person who aligns their every thought, self-talk, word, and action to the person he wants to become; an aligned person lives consciously from moment to moment, deliberately finding joy in everyday, so-called 'mundane' routines and activities because they know that as long as breath exists in them, they are deserving of and will receive their purpose – and so, an aligned person has found an excellent reason to live, and looks forward to another day of being themselves: an aligned person.

An aligned person is someone who cannot be beaten; this is someone that knows they are deserving of everything good – which invites more good to align in their life experience. Hence, an aligned person is more charismatic, attractive, practical, powerful, and appealing than millions who have not achieved this alignment. In this state of alignment, there is no such thing as impossible, no dream too big, and no desire too great.

How to align, you ask? Let me introduce you to the Living in Alignment Approach: work on unresolved thoughts, and then incorporate the resolved thoughts into action. To understand this better and align beautifully, realize the following first: You are a three-fold being consisting of the energy body (physical), energy mind (non-physical), and energy soul (metaphysical). These three entities are in the creation business. Every minute of every day, you create and turn over a new manifestation leaf as quickly as right now, in this present moment, as you absorb yourself into the beautiful words on this page.

In this life you are living, the process of creation starts with a single thought – a clear belief that a desire or goal you want to achieve or make happen in your lifetime WILL happen no matter what! The belief that you really can have, do, or be anything begins the process of Law of Attraction (LOA).

LOA in action: 1) Align, 2) then Ask, 3) then Allow! Notice alignment comes first before asking and allowing, showing you how essential it is to build the STRONGEST foundation of Living in Alignment from the inside out. Do not rush the process, for if you're not willing to look like a foolish beginner, you will never become a graceful master.

And so, alignment is where the MAGIC happens because choosing your life (through your choice of thoughts, self-talk, words, and actions) is courageous, and to be exceptional requires courage. With courageous alignment, you become one with your desires.

Throughout this glorious journey and process, I became intensely aware of aligning my being with every chosen thought, and every word was deliberately spoken. Inexplicable things began to happen, and the world around me began to change.

This process may sound effortless, but as the saying goes, 'nothing good comes easy' – so I knew that the harder I was finding it, the more of it I had to do! My motivation came from knowing that this solid practice is purely for my benefit. With this knowledge in mind, I persevered each new day to align myself with the person I wish to be (fully understanding that the person is not OUT THERE, she is here with me, already, now – INSIDE OF ME ALREADY). I decided to spend my days creating a life with complete positivity using the Living in Alignment approach. Through this daily practice, I felt INCREDIBLE about myself and noticeable shifts, synchronicities, and coincidences began to shape my new life.

I soon realized that nothing, absolutely nothing, is random. I believe we have taken the term 'coincidence' to mean 'accidental' when in fact, the word 'coincide' comes from geometry – when two angles perfectly coincide with each other, on purpose; so, a coincidence is not an accident AT ALL – it is synchronicity that was meant to happen perfectly.

This great realization inspired me. The more I experienced these co-incidences (attracted due to my daily actions of alignment), the more my days became an enjoyable, creative time to keep shedding old thoughts and beliefs and build a vibrant, better-quality day, mindset, and, best of all, being.

In a short time, doors that were once shut finally began to open – the alignments (energy) I created with my thoughts, self-talk, words, and actions started coming true! I became a happy, healthy person who consciously aligned her energy with her desires. I became someone who so quickly manifested things she thought about with intense emotion and genuine feeling. I realized nothing is more accurate and real than this process of aligning your energies to the goal of the person you wish to become.

Remember throughout your life: the goal is to be so well-aligned with your top intention/s that nothing can mess with your vibration.

The 4 Realizations to Alignment

1. Thought is the first level of creation. You get to choose your thoughts – HOW COOL IS THAT?
2. Next comes the spoken or written word. Every word you speak is creative and brings creative energy into your universe. To muster the courage to speak the idea you have just formed, remember that your words come back to you, multiplied – tenfold! You were MEANT to have that idea so that you can ACT on it for the greater good of the universe! So, talk big, for you are limiting yourself if you talk small. Your aura cleanses and heightens when you speak your desires and dreams into existence. Avoid dialogue of unwanted experiences, situations, or results. Let your words speak life!
3. Next comes action: the real and natural game-changer. Actions are words moving. If you want your life to take off, begin at once to check every thought, word, and action that does not fall in harmony with your alignment.
4. When you have a thought that is not in alignment with your highest vision, change to a new thought then and there. When you say something that is out of alignment with your grandest idea, make a note not to say something like that again. When you do something misaligned with your best intention, decide to make that the last time. And make it right with whoever was involved, if you can.

The key to reprogramming my subconscious mind was through repetition of deliberately designed, empowering alignments (thoughts, words and actions) full of love and emotion! By choosing encouraging thoughts, words, and actions, crystal-clear visualization, and feeling genuine sentiments of alignment, success, health, and positivity, my subconscious got reprogrammed (just as it is designed to). I became ready, willing – and most influential of all – PROACTIVE to make those positive thoughts, words, and feelings come true for me.

I conjured up the emotions I wanted to feel when I was that aligned person I wanted to be, and it became mine. It had to come true; it is the law. Knowing how the laws of the universe work and knowing without a shadow of a doubt that they exist to serve me opened up a whole new universe within me, first in my mind (because life is 90% mental) and second in my physical reality. I began to understand that giving WAY MORE regard to the inner life changes the outer physical experience drastically and quickly.

When I began the process of aligning myself with the person I want to be, I had many great realizations and revelations that permanently changed the way I view and live my life:

- The Living in Alignment process is a vast 'overcoming to become'. You must 'unlearn to learn'. In other words, you must make all the mistakes to get over them before you can realize precisely WHO you want to be and, therefore, WHAT alignment (new thoughts, better self-talk, actual action) it takes to get there.

- I realized alignment requires tremendous mental effort. It entails constant, moment-to-moment awareness of your every thought, word, and deed, and conscious choice-making daily. Only after a while does it start to become really fun living consciously, because you then acquire a deep knowing that the universe is guiding you (and cheering you on and applauding you! Yeah, it really is!) while you take the necessary actions (alignment) to become the new you.

- When you undertake this challenge, you will find out you've spent half your life unconscious or out of alignment with what you desire. You were unaware you could choose alignment! ("Seriously?! You can CHOOSE alignment?!" Yes, yes, you can.) When you decide to align your human self with your energetic self (your aligned and, therefore, vibrational self), you will undoubtedly experience the benefits of Living in Alignment. This means you will enjoy all your present moments, acquire self-confidence and self-esteem, achieve your purpose, and experience fulfilling, happy relationships, amongst a hundred more benefits.

- The universe does its 'thing' where it aligns you with people, things, and situations that match your vibration. The higher you vibrate in this energy of living in alignment with the person you really want to become, the universe will keep on sending you gems to help you on this energetic journey: you will automatically meet like-minded souls, see more of the people you love in your life, you will do more of the things you love daily, and you will attract highly beneficial things for your well-being.

- When I conjured up a good idea, I learnt that the most practical and effective way to bring that idea to fruition is to align my thoughts, feelings, and actions with that idea, coupled with creating that vision and desired feeling within myself. From there, I intentionally, knowingly, and intelligently invited the Law of Vibration and the Law of Attraction into my experience just by having an inner thought – an inner event.

- Know that the laws are real, absolute, fundamental, and natural, and exist solely to work in your favor if you choose to experience their power. Use them!

The process of alignment requires you to trust yourself and your decisions. Please consider these questions while in the pursuit of Living in Your Alignment. Be honest in your answers, and keep working on asking yourself these questions if your answers to them aren't 100% absolute:

Since self-trust is a daily practice, to work on trusting yourself more and more every day, ask and answer:

- Am I trusting my daily choices and decisions?
- How often and why do I doubt my choices?
- Am I willing to examine and let go of those thoughts and feelings that no longer serve me?
- Do I trust my new, imaginative ideas?
- Am I listening to my heart, as it is telling me the truth of how I feel?
- Do I believe my life is unfolding perfectly at the perfect time?

- Do I trust that I exist for a reason and that everything is happening for my highest good?
- Am I willing to admit that I have created some energy blocks within myself (from lousy life experiences) that I now want to unblock?
- Where am I waiting to receive myself?
- Do I believe that only good lies ahead of me?

An old phrase says that when you feel stuck in one place, you are given the time and space to heal and release the baggage you can't carry to your next stop. This is your time to heal. To think. To re-align. Do this by TRUSTING the perspectives that everything in your life is happening FOR you, for your greater good – and then, do the inner work of asking the deep questions and fine-tuning/rewiring/reprogramming your sub-conscious mind to make you believe that this life was built and designed specifically for you.

Do what is required. No shortcuts.

Six Valuable Call-to-Actions

- All that said, right now, you can do nothing except relax! Relax, and everything comes; relax, and you start vibrating. The more relaxed you are, the better you are at everything. In fact, your only and most important job is to relax, have fun, and do things that make you feel really good so that you begin activating the Law of Attraction and draw those things to you as if you were born a powerful magnet (you were! It is a fact!)
- Relax without worrying about the past or future because they do not exist. The present is all you have—trust that this moment is perfect because the present is always perfect. Does this trust bring you relief? It should. If not, you must do more inner work to trust yourself.
- Attracting is the MOST fundamental act you can play around with while you choose to live your life and co-create with the

universe consciously, but instead of waiting in anticipation for an end goal, you need to live in the moment. With that said, the trick to activating the Law of Attraction as you live each moment of your life is to make your current reality as 'perfect' as possible. To do so, feel good about yourself and where you are right now. In this feel-good state, your body produces euphoric vibrations needed to follow your greatest ambitions. The only thing we are born with is our bodies, so our lifelong job is to take care of our thoughts that are produced from this body. Our most important job is to feel good in our bodies and minds. Alignment helps you to feel good and keep feeling good! Hopefully, you will take home the message that to heal our planet and heal others, you need only look after yourself more. It will always start and end with you.

- When you choose to feel good, your brain picks up everything to 1) retire old thoughts and dreams and 2) bring forth your new, current thoughts, ideas, and ambitions. It would be best if you looked forward to where you want to be while not complaining about where you are because the present moment is all we ever have, and it rarely asks much of us other than to be ourselves and enjoy being ourselves. The alignment will come only when you are being who you are and when you love the person you already are, the wonderful person you have created thus far! APPRECIATE YOURSELF, because what you appreciate appreciates you.

- You are always exactly where you're supposed to be, so practice enjoying the moment in front of you and the moment about to unfold in front of you. The grass may be green where you water it, but it is also green right here. "Paradise" and "heaven" are not 'out there' – they are on earth. If you want to see paradise, sim- ply look around and feel it. This is an utterly critical perspective because, in most cases, life doesn't honor where we want to go until we appreciate where we are now. Remember: the goal is not to be aligned at this minute—the goal is to enjoy the journey of being an aligned person, because that means you are living in and enjoying the moment.

- NOTICE the ideas that spring into your mind and write them down! (The biggest lie you tell yourself is, "I will remember that thought.") As you think, you build ideas, and a massive part of self-trust is trusting an imaginative idea when you receive one—most notably, trust that you were destined to have that idea. You were! Did you know that ideas come one size too big so that we can grow into them? Now that you know, are you awake enough to catch them? Do you trust your idea enough to pursue it? All achievements have their beginning in an idea! My book, Euphoric Living, began with a single idea in mind and is now published and in people's hands worldwide.

So, please, do not wait for 'tomorrow'. What action step/s are you taking today to live in perfect alignment?

Bonus:
Freewriting Call-to-Actions

1. With great conviction, copy and write out the following alignment statements to help begin the process of reprogramming your sub-conscious – or better yet, create your own depending on how you are feeling, and use the specifics of what you want to attract in your life using alignment.
2. Vibe with and delight in the positive sensations and feelings of this magic. Make your writing and beliefs in them strong, intense, and euphoric. How you do this one thing is how you do everything. Treat this with excellence and see how your life changes. Most importantly, enjoy the time you spend doing this fun attraction/alignment exercise.

Alignment Statements

- I am aligned, ambitious, and excited to make today magnificent!
- I protect and focus my aura with ease and grace.

- Everything is always aligning in my favor!
- I have learnt so much. I am a graceful master.
- Life supports my strongest desires, and I am well taken care of.
- I am becoming aware of how my thoughts, words, and actions shape my life.
- I flow quickly and effortlessly to what is already mine.
- I am in synchrony and tune with the world around me.
- All my intentions are entirely, perfectly, naturally, and miraculously flowing to me!
- I prioritize the activities that get me to where I want to be
- I prioritize activities that help me become who I want to be.
- PERFECT ALIGNMENT IS MY BIRTHRIGHT!

I hope this chapter inspires you to come into alignment and make long-lasting changes to your well-being and our world, and I hope you will happily share the process with others to help them heal and grow.

All that said, the new trend is to take personal development too seriously, which can take the fun out of everyday life. I believe that the most loving act possible is to laugh, have fun, and be yourself. Be so you that you can enhance the world. And then, make this wisdom go viral.

To your utmost success, and with best wishes, believe me,
Shyla

About the Author

Shyla Melwani is a wellness warrior on a mission to help others transform their lives through the power of self-care. Her experience of years of living in a sick, unhealthy, and overweight body encouraged her to explore the benefits of a healing journey, inspiring her to publish her first book, Euphoric Living, and spread to man the knowledge of healing and loving the body from the inside out. The interactive workbook empowers people to prioritize their mental well-being and embrace self-care as the new healthcare to optimize work, body, mind, and spirit on a cellular level.

Shyla's mission is to encourage people to look after themselves more, so she published a book suitable for all humankind, hoping to continue and fortify conversations about self-care as the new healthcare!

Shyla's valuable take-home message is simple: take care of yourself, because you are the key to saving the world.

Author Contact Information

Email: Melwani.s27@gmail.com
Website: www.shylamelwani.com

You Are Worthy of Your Own Happiness

by Tri Nuraini

*The journey of loving myself has been a
long journey, not a destination.
It is a lifelong journey.*

-Tri Nuraini

spent most of my life focusing on what's missing. I was always looking for answers from the outside, but I never found what I was looking for. I looked for inner peace and happiness, but never found it. That all changed the moment I made a decision to focus on myself. I stopped trying to find something externally and at that moment, inner peace found me. Happiness found me. Purpose found me. And I realized that the life that I wanted to create was right in front of me.

It all started when I turned thirty a few years ago. I remember that day so clearly because I truly felt lost. Although I had an amazing career, great friends, and a loving family, I felt empty. I wasn't sure why I felt like this because it seemed I had everything. A fabulous support group and an exciting life. I traveled to beautiful places and had many adventures, but I felt so alone.

At this point, most of my friends had gotten married and had kids. It seemed like they were moving on with their lives, and mine felt like it had stalled. I kept getting in and out of relationships, but most of them were unhealthy ones. In many of my relationships, I felt like I was just holding on because I didn't want to feel alone. I repeated this pattern. The men I dated were not the type I wanted to develop a lifelong relationship with. I kept dating unavailable guys and they weren't that nice. I often felt like I was emotionally abused, and most often, the men just left me.

I fell into a deep sadness, feeling unworthy. I felt like I didn't deserve a beautiful love and a loving life partner. I felt alone, and I was scared. Truth be told, I felt like a failure, like I was a disappointment to my family. I cried inside.

Deep in my heart, I felt that I would not be truly happy until I found someone who would truly stand by me. I felt like I would continue to disappoint my parents if I didn't marry. It felt like my "duty" as a woman was not completed without getting married and having kids. I often felt inferior and ashamed, constantly comparing myself with others. It was a very hard time for me.

I wondered, "Oh my, how did I get here?"

I found myself drowning in a sea of fears. Fears of loneliness. Fears of rejection. Fears of being left out. And most importantly, the worst fear of all, the fear of spending the rest of my life alone. These fears haunted me.

I kept a brave face through this period. From the outside I looked fine. People saw me as a happy, successful woman, yet inside I was crying. I could not face myself. I felt unworthy of my own happiness.

The realization came at work. At that time I was managing a team of ten people in my company. I wanted to be friends with my teammates, and this created tension since I was supposed to be in charge. I was so busy "pleasing" them, trying so hard to be loved. I wanted to look "nice", so that they would be nice and indeed, love me. In short, I became a people pleaser. I did everything for everyone and everyone on my team did like me. And then, one day, I made a mistake, and overnight my image as a "good" boss disappeared. I was shunned by my teammates, they didn't talk to me anymore outside work, and they didn't even want to have lunch with me anymore.

I lost friends. I lost the feeling of security when I was "liked and loved", and finally, I fell into the abyss of prolonged sadness. I was overwhelmed with feelings of confusion and sadness. At first I blamed them, as I wondered why they were so hard on me. In the end, though, I turned the blame onto myself. Why did I make this mistake? Why was I so stupid that I had fallen into a situation like this?

I felt depressed for months. It was hard for me to sleep, and every day felt like a torture. No matter how much I tried to numb away the feelings with entertainment and traveling, I came back feeling empty. I fell deep, all the way to rock bottom. I lost friends.

I was so alone. I was scared.

It took a while for me to realize that all of this was due to my people pleasing tendencies. I spent so much time trying so hard to please others and to get affection from them that I never even considered what I needed. I began to examine my relationships and my circle of friends. I discovered that the root of my problems was not the people around me or the situation I was in, but rather myself. There is a part of me that was always craving to be noticed and loved by others. The part of me that was hurt and always felt deprived. The constant pressure of trying to please everyone else, trying to be liked, made me forget all about what I needed.

A Journey of Loving Myself

I decided to go on a transformational journey. I was not going to spend the rest of my life in these negative behavior patterns. I looked deeply inward and realized that all of these failed relationships and broken friendships were a lesson for me. I decided to learn the lesson, and I can honestly say that I am glad that I had to go through all the heartache because that is what brought me here, to the most heartfelt journey of my life. A deep inner journey of healing and growth.

This was a watershed moment for me. The moment I made the decision to get to know myself better and to understand who I really was helped me immensely. I decided that I wanted to find love and peace within, not from others.

The Dalai Lama once said, you can't make people happy if you're not happy. I resonate strongly with this quote because if you are not happy, you will not be able to find it outside of yourself, and you also will not be able to help others find their happiness.

As I went on my journey to get to know myself, I saw my patterns. I was so busy looking for love from a partner and from other people, always trying to get love and attention from outside that I had neglected myself. My efforts at trying to "be nice and do good" so that others would treat me well left me exhausted, and it was never-ending. I had spent a lifetime trying to fill my glass from my partners, friends, colleagues, and even strangers. And when I was mistreated, I fell into a deep pit of sorrow. I was busy "giving" to others until I finally emptied myself. I gave love not from a glass that was full, but mostly from an empty glass. That was when I discovered self love.

Self love is about filling our glass with great affection without depending on other people or self-achievement. It's nurturing unconditional love for ourselves. Treating ourselves with love and compassion. It's that simple.

Self Love

The key to moving towards your very best life is to practice self love. Doing small things throughout the day to take care of yourself can be a game changer.

Begin the practice by being gentle with yourself. Stop judging yourself when you make mistakes. Simply learn the lesson you need to learn and move on. Be kind to yourself during rough times in life. Learn to receive compliments with open arms and celebrate your accomplishments without guilt. Accept and forgive yourself with all your scars and flaws.

Self-love is not selfish. We can still love others and ourselves at the same time. Happiness is no longer determined by the outside world, but from ourselves, so that in the end we can make the people we love even better. Because we give from a full cup.

Step by Step to Jump Start Your Self-Love Journey

Ok, so you know you need to practice self love. The question remains, "How?"

The moment I decided to focus on myself, like many of you, I went all the way. I took courses, joined an educational platform to have access to transformational courses. I read many books. I started meditating regularly. I truly enjoyed myself in the process. However, if I could sum up what would be the simplest way to approach, these steps gave a greatest impact in the beginning of my journey:

Step 1: Being Present

Breathing in, I calm body and mind.
Breathing out, I smile.
Dwelling in the present moment, I know this is the only moment.
~Thich Nhat Hanh

Yes, being present, fully grounded in the present moment. I believe many of us see this as a very familiar concept, however it is always nice to be reminded of the importance of it. Being fully in the present liberates us from anxiety of the past and the future, and we can then live the life that we want.

Meditation in passive and active ways is definitely very helpful. Other ideas to become fully present in this moment is to pray, exercise, play an instrument, walk in nature, listen to music, dance, and do breath work. Basically anything that helps you to feel joyful will help you move into the present moment.

I personally love a grounding meditation, as taught by Jeffrey Allen. He teaches a grounding meditation, and all you do is simply imagine our grounding chord like a beam of light, tree roots, or waterfalls from us to the center of the earth. To this day, I begin each day this way. This simple practice helps me to feel grounded every day.

Step 2: Cultivating Gratitude

If your dream is the seed, action is the water to grow the seed,
sunlight is the consistency, gratitude is the fertilizer.
~Lisa Nichols

Living in gratitude is indeed a beautiful place to be. Practicing gratitude allows us to embrace the beauty of life in every moment. The benefits of gratitude include reducing stress as well as having a positive outlook in life and attracting even more good things in life.

For me, it was when I started gratitude journaling and learned to detach myself from material possessions through minimalism that I felt the shift so strongly. I have been doing this practice for over five years, and I have never stopped. I might skip some days, but I always come back. All you need to do is sit down and write a list of the things you are grateful for. When days are hard, when you're not feeling it, it is actually the best day to journal. It is essential to keep counting your blessings no matter what. And when you do, you will see how your energy shifts instantly.

Happiness is a choice. And gratitude is how you step into it.

Step 3: Acceptance

> *Happiness can exist only in acceptance.*
> ~George Orwell

Accepting our feelings and all the experiences that are coming to us gracefully helps to keep us balanced. Listening to our emotions allows us to learn about ourselves and helps us to develop a deep inner resilience and inner peace.

I found that I used to simply deny my feelings so much in the past. When I finally learned (and continuously learn) to accept whatever feelings and experiences come into my life, I was able to process them instead of just burying them inside. They are there as part of a beautiful human experience in this lifetime. The key is to honor our feelings, embrace them, and then let them go.

I learned to listen to my body when difficult emotions arise. The best way I have found to do this is through meditation, prayer, and journaling. There is no fixed method to practice. Simply find a way to listen to your thoughts and emotions. For me, I use many different methods. Sometimes I just wanted to cry, other times I needed to journal, and still others I found meditation was the doorway inwards. Another great method that really works for me is to take a long bath. I give space for myself to process the emotion that comes and it has made all the difference.

I ask myself lovingly, "What would support me at this moment? How can I process this emotion?"

One of my favorite prayers to touch acceptance within me is through the Serenity prayer:

> *God, grant me the serenity to accept things that I can not change,*
> *the courage to change the things I can,*
> *and the wisdom to know the difference.*

Step 4: Forgiveness

Forgive yourself for not knowing what you didn't know before you learned it.
~Maya Angelou

Self-forgiveness is definitely one of the most challenging parts of the journey. It hasn't been easy to forgive myself, but I also know it's not difficult at the same time.

Self-forgiveness is a process of meeting yourself fully, and embracing all the sides of yourself that you don't even want to see. Forgiving ourselves means learning to accept our shortcomings, let go of the burdens, and walk with courage, gratitude, and faith in the future.

It is really hard to describe what self-forgiveness actually means. One of the practices that created a tremendous shift in me is *The Mirror Work Exercise* by Lisa Nichols. It is when we literally face ourselves in the mirror, saying that we are proud, forgive, and commit to ourselves. Fill in the blanks for each of these statements below. Use seven different things to fill in each statement so that you are speaking out 21 statements in the mirror each morning.

The Mirror Exercise

Fill in the blanks seven times for each statement:
I am proud of myself that I…
I forgive myself for…
I commit to myself that…

This practice will change your life. It certainly changed mine. There were days that I would just cry throughout the practice, saying all the things that I want to forgive myself for. It was quite painful at first until one day, I felt a huge release, and I felt like a weight had been lifted. Or perhaps I simply put the weight down. In that moment I began to smile, and everything felt light and easy. When it happened I thought, "Oh, is this what self-forgiveness feels like?" I also realized in that moment that I am worthy of my happiness.

Self-love is a deep journey inwards, and it's a beautiful one. Through the course of life, we surely will always have our ups and downs. Well, guess what, same thing with our journey in self-love. I found myself, just like everybody else, not immune to life's ups and down. Nevertheless, no matter what happens, I learned to see things from a different perspective, and I know in my heart I can always come back to love myself. My life now has changed forever. I am happier and healthier than ever.

Final Words

In this journey, I found my mission, my voice in the world, and it became my spiritual path. Fast forward to today, as I am writing this chapter, I just published my first book, where I'm writing about my journey in finding self-love and providing guidance for those who are interested in following a similar path. I wrote my book especially for women, to support them on their journey. I wrote the book last year, not even realizing at the time that it would be a huge part of my development.

Early this year I decided to enroll in a life coaching course, where I studied to be an extraordinary life coach. After 12 years of career in the corporate world, I fully transitioned my career to fully live my purpose. I became a full-time life coach.

Everything in my life is unfolding beautifully. I have never been happier and more fulfilled. I speak about my journey in communities, I create workshops, I grow my own community, and I have many projects in the pipeline.

I am creating the life that I love.

I know in my heart I want to help more women in this journey of life. My mission is to empower women to break free from anxiety, find their purpose, love themselves unconditionally, and live the most fulfilling and joyful life they desire.

I am so grateful for this journey. I am worthy of my happiness. And so are you. Take this in fully, let it truly sink in, "You are worthy of your happiness."

With love,
Tri

About the Author

---🌣---

Tri Nuraini, also called Inuk, is a Certified Life Coach who focuses on self-love and purpose based in Jakarta, Indonesia. Her first book which was just released recently, *I'm Worthy – Menerima Diri Sepenuhnya Tanpa Tapi* is the first book of *The Love Journey Series* that she wrote based on her reflections of her personal reflection and journey of self transformation.

Tri graduated in Management from University of Indonesia and Masters in Marketing Communications University of Birmingham. Nevertheless, after 12 years of career in Business and Marketing, she finally decided to fulfill her calling to become a full-time Life Coach after obtaining Life Coach certification from Mindvalley. She believes that her main mission in the world is "to empower women to discover their true purpose, love themselves unconditionally, and live the most fulfilling life."

Currently she is also still teaching as a lecturer at the Communication Studies program at a private university in Jakarta. She is also active as a Mindvalley Regional Ambassador for Indonesia, building a loving community that she cherishes. On the weekends she can be found playing tennis, swing-dancing, playing the piano, or spending time with her nephews.

Author Contact Information

---🌣---

Website: https://trinuraini.com/
Email: hello@trinuraini.com

It's OK Not to Be Okay!

by Nolan Pillay

Instead of going through Pain, focus on GROWING through Pain.

~Nolan Pillay

woke up in the hospital with the doctors pumping from my stomach a whole lot of tablets I had swallowed earlier. Why was I trying to find the easy way out?

The simple answer, I was too embarrassed and concerned about what society would think about me and my family. I was worried that they would call me a failure and look down on my family. This is unfortunately what happens in close knit communities.

Let's go back, it was the year 1989. I was excelling in my sports at school, in fact I was Sportsman of the year for five years in a row. I could have become a top footballer, basketball player, or even an athlete, but the country system did not allow a person of color to go past provincial colors. This meant that I was not allowed to progress to my actual skill level, just the level they deemed acceptable for people of color.

This is the way it has been my entire life. I recall fighting against the Apartheid system for my entire life. It was very hard to deal with it without becoming bitter, but I refused to stay a victim or have a self-pity mindset. I believe this attitude got me to where I am now. I somehow instinctively adopted a growth mindset even when I was struggling to succeed in a system that was rigged to keep me in the same position people of color were always in.

When I was in school, I believed that I was a bright student, and my results reflected that. I did not have any failing grades, my teachers were all happy with me, and I was quite proactive in my studying. We formed study groups in our matriculation year and our preliminary tests proved that I was on the right track. Being such a confident young man, I went into the exams ready and wanting to get it over with. I felt confident and I believed that all the papers that I wrote went well. And then, finally, my exams were over.

I was looking forward to seeing my results. Back then, we had to wait for the results, and they were actually published in the newspaper believe it or not. The day the grades were due, we had to wait until midnight for the paper to be released. I eventually got my copy of the newspaper, and eagerly looked for my name. I started to go up and down in search of my name, but I couldn't find it. I checked a few more times and still nothing. I called my friend over and asked him to check for me, and he said, "Sorry your name is not here."

My heart dropped. This could mean only one thing that… I had failed. My heart skipped a few beats, and I started to feel really sad. All around me, my friends were celebrating, and there I was, standing there in tears. I decided to get a grip on the news, to give myself a moment to take it in. I decided I would wait until the next day to visit the school and speak to the teachers, I was not going to give up!

The next morning, I walked to the school and waited for the Principal to come in. Finally, he arrived and greeted me. I greet him back and expand to him what my query is. At this point I could sense that he was aware that I had failed, but he was trying to make me feel better by going through his list. Eventually he said, I am sorry, but you did not make it. I remember feeling a stabbing sensation in my heart. The news really hits me now. I put my head down in shame and left the office.

I decided to walk home. It was about 200-300 meters away. All I could think about while walking home was killing myself. My only thought was suicide. I got home, in tears. Everything seemed so hopeless. I didn't know what to do. Before I could change my mind, I grabbed a whole handful of tablets, a glass of water, and went into my "sibling shared" room, where I proceeded to take the pills. I was ready to die.

I don't recall anything after that. The next memory I have is of waking up in hospital with my stomach being pumped to remove the tablets. Even more embarrassing is the questions that follow and the self-pity words which I did not want to hear at the time. They kept asking me "Why…?" As if they didn't know. I felt so embarrassed, absolutely humiliated.

I had no choice but to face the public. I began to go out again, at first with my head down, but somehow I adjusted and after some time, I started to walk proudly again.

That same year, I started working as a sweeper in a factory. My job entailed mopping the floors around the machine area. I was grateful for this job as without a matric, I had very few choices. I was simply happy to get a salary.

After six months at the job, I had a remarkable experience. I remember it so clearly, even after all this time. I was working a 12-hour night shift, spending my shift packing boxes. Suddenly, I heard a voice that was crystal clear. I looked around to see where the voice was coming from, but I didn't see anyone. I kept looking and realized that there was no one around me.

Still, the voice persisted. The voice asked me boldly "Nolan, is this where you want to be for the rest of your Life?"

My immediate answer was "No." That was an awakening moment for me as I made a choice right there. I made the choice that this job would not define me, failing would not define me. I would succeed and to do so, I knew I had to take massive action. And that is what I did. I started to work on weekends in addition to my normal hours. I was able to save enough money to fund my studies. This allowed me to grow within the company, to the point of becoming a Senior Technical Engineering Buyer. This is just one example of how a simple decision combined with rapid action can be a game changer in your life.

I can tell you this much, it was not an easy journey. I can also tell you that all of the obstacles that came with were actually a blessing to me, because overcoming those obstacles gave me confidence in myself. They became a blessing to me as they allowed me to learn and grow even more. If you go back to the quote *"Instead of going through pain, focus on growing through pain,"* you will realize that I practice what I speak about.

Hang ten, the journey gets even better. I had reached the peak in my career and became a SAP consultant, traveling the world, earning a good salary, enjoying the perks of being a contractor. But that wasn't to be all for me. In June 2019, I had another awakening moment in my life. I went through as one of my mentors would say, "My Beautiful Destruction". I started to see how humans behave in corporate, how they learned to become inhumane, and how they eventually would get to the point where they felt free to trample on anyone to get ahead. They were willing to do anything just to move higher within the company and gain popularity.

I saw myself as the victim when racism was used against me but by this point in my life, I had grown and had the freedom to speak my mind. This eventually led to me leaving the company, which allowed me to move out of an extremely toxic environment.

At first, I felt like I was going to go back into victim mode, but when I looked deeper into myself I realized that this was a sign from my Higher Power. To use the tools I had learned through the adversity I had suffered in my life. So I changed my mindset. I started to take all the negatives and convert every situation into a positive one.

How did I achieve this you may wonder? At this point I was on a journey of self-discovery and learned from the legendary late Bob Proctor about the power of my thoughts and how to convert negative thinking into positive ones. I made this into a daily habit and used it to my benefit, as I had a lot of healing and forgiving to do and needed to fix myself first. I looked back at my childhood and the values I was brought up with and asked myself if those values were in line with who I had become. The answer was no, those values no longer resonated with me. So I asked myself, "Okay, so what next then Nolan?"

I started to re-evaluate myself by filling in the gaps on who I would like to become, how I could make a difference to others, and how I could become the best version of myself. This was a time of deep soul searching. As I looked back on my childhood journey, I realized that I had been very affected by my background of poverty. Life was never easy for us. The little my parents earned was used to take care of us and provide food and shelter. There were some days and weeks when we did not have electricity due to lack of funds.

Our circumstances were due to the Apartheid system in South Africa. Being a person of color, there were no opportunities for people to get good jobs or further their studies. We were segregated by race groups and put into areas where it was difficult to access the city center or shops. We were limited in all ways. We didn't even have access to knowledge, as this was before the internet and the only way to get information was to go to the library, and these were not accessible to us. We were disadvantaged in every way.

Through all of this, I learned not to allow the circumstances to dictate who I should be. Although the Apartheid system in South Africa was not our fault, it did keep us in a victim mentality. I am grateful that I learned early on that I had to refuse to stay in a victim or self-pity mindset. Changing my mindset was my ticket to the future and to a better life.

I wanted to share a great tool I used when I was making the momentous decision to leave corporate life. I did an exercise where I had to write down the values that resonated with me and as I made my list, the one that stood out the most for me was the word humanity. I wondered, what does humanity mean to me? As I considered it, I thought that perhaps my purpose in life was linked to humanity. I dug deep to understand this aspect of myself and what humanity really meant.

At this point in life, I was coaching students and I enjoyed adding value to their lives. I loved seeing the smile on their faces when they had a moment of awakening during our coaching sessions. Many of the students lived in rural areas, with little or no access to the internet, so they could not go online and access resources that could help them. They truly appreciated the fact that I was making the time to coach them and guide them. I loved it too. So much, in fact, that at that time, I was doing all this work pro-bono. I loved doing this work, as I was learning from my students as much as they were learning from me. Plus I was learning all about myself.

In the very same year that I left the corporate world, I decided to re-launch my company StraightTalkWithNolan. At the launch, a friend of mine invited three deaf people to speak, with the help of an interpreter to help the hearing audience. These speakers inspired me, and eventually helped me to find my life's mission.

One of the speakers, Mrs. Deaf South Africa 2019, asked me and the audience a question that I know will stick with me for the rest of my life. She asked, "What if all of you cannot hear and I am the only one who can hear, who is the one with the disability?" Wow! This struck a nerve, it hit me right in my heart and I can still recall how I felt at the time. At that moment, the value of humanity had come alive for me, and I realized that no matter what disability a person has, they are still human. She changed my perspective that day, and I owe her a debt of gratitude I can never repay. She has passed away now, may she rest in peace, but her influence over me will last my entire lifetime and through my work, even longer I hope.

As I heard those words, I promised myself that I would do whatever it takes to make a difference to the Deaf community. And I have. My purpose of serving humanity has become a reality. Today, we have collaborated with the deaf community and we will be summiting the highest mountain in Africa, Mount Kilimanjaro. The funds we raise from the initiative will go towards giving the gift of hearing to a child by purchasing hearing aids and cochlear implants, which will change their life. This is priceless! The initiative is the first project that our foundation, *Be the BEST Version of YOURSELF,* will start with, but we will continue on after this initiative.

We plan on serving humanity in various ways and every year, we will pick a different cause and work towards it.

My tip for you is to do this simple values exercise. Simply sit down and write out a list of your values. Look at the list and decide which ones are most important to you, and then check if they fit into your present life. See how you can do things that will bring your values into your day to day living. This is the way to live a purposeful life, to leave a legacy, and to serve humanity. It's a beautiful way to build your life. Dig deep within and find the answers, they will come to you, the same way it did for me. Then get to work building it and as you do, keep this message in mind: "You must find that place inside yourself where nothing is impossible."

Talking about values and finding one's purpose, a company called Mindvalley popped into my life in the year 2020. Out of the blue, I saw an ad for a course called Be Extraordinary and I thought to myself, yes, this is so me. I signed up for the course immediately, and eventually joined the platform so that I could access all the information there. I am so grateful and thankful to this educational company. I use it to get my daily dose for personal development. I suggest you find a personal development platform that resonates with you so that you, too, can get daily inspiration. It is important to keep learning and growing in order to become the best version of yourself.

I found a technique called the Silva Method, which was a true game changer for me. I love the mediation techniques the course offered, but the most impactful thing for me was something called the "Three Scenes Technique", for healing and manifesting what you desire in your life. I learned the technique, not realizing that it would soon play a role in saving my life.

You see, in January 2021, I became very ill with covid-pneumonia. I was shocked to get so sick because I was very fit and active and I thought I had learned all the techniques I needed to overcome any obstacle that was thrown my way. When I first got sick, I wasn't worried, figuring I would get better after a few days. Instead, my symptoms got worse and worse and I ended up in the hospital, in the Intensive Care Unit, for thirteen days. When I was admitted to the hospital, I had 58% oxygen levels. While I was in the hospital, I used the Three Scenes Technique from the Silva Method, and I believe it was the reason I got better. I believe it saved my life. I was so inspired by how powerful this practice and how effective it was at helping me heal, that I ended up writing a book about it called, *My COVID Journey*, available on Amazon. If you lost a loved one through covid and would like to know what they experienced, you should check out my book. It will help you to understand the impact of the disease, and it will help you reach closure and find some peace to move on.

In the book, I share some mind hacks and techniques that I used on myself to get through the hospital stay and to get better. As I mentioned, the Three Scenes Technique was the most important one I practiced. I did it five times each day while I was in hospital. I wanted to share the technique with you. This is a very small snippet, but will give you an idea of the technique.

The Three Scenes Technique

Scene 1 – In the first scene, imagine a big mental screen and envision what is currently happening in your life, the current situation. In the hospital, I would envision the mental screen in front of me and portray the pain I am going through. There is no need to dramatize it more as I am experiencing this first-hand.

Scene 2 – In the second scene, play out how you will resolve the situation. In the hospital, I would play out what I am going to do from my side to help with my recovery. I imagined the doctors and modern medicine playing their role, the nurses doing their best and me, trusting the process and having a positive attitude, I imagined the high-flowing oxygen playing its part as it is my lifeline. My strategy to help the process is to sit up and sleep in a chair to be able to breathe better. This chair became a famous chair in the hospital.

Scene 3 – In the third and final scene, imagine the situation fully resolved the way you want it to be. In the hospital, I would imagine that I was completely well, fully recovered, at home and that I was enjoying being myself again. I even went so far as to visualize myself playing in the yard with my grandchildren. I am fit and healthy, doing daily walks with my wife around the dam, just enjoying the peacefulness of nature.

*****

Earlier in this chapter, I spoke about my Suicide episode, and now I have shared my covid experience. In the first example, I was actually trying to kill myself but in the second, I was fighting to live. How strange is life that it tests us in this way?

These were examples of how I turned a painful experience into a success story. Michael Beckwith speaks about the Kensho moment, which are those moments in which you experience temporary pain that drives personal growth. I have come to understand that these moments define us and can change the course of our life if we let them.

My latest online course called "*Battling to Breathe*" speaks about mental wellness, depression, suicide, limiting beliefs, and how we as humans go through life allowing ourselves to feel suffocated. The inspiring thing about the program is that it speaks about my life experiences and how I learnt to overcome obstacles to get to where I am now. Remember obstacles will always come your way, but being consciously aware of them and learning how to deal with them is the answer to becoming the best version of yourself.

Why did I come up with this program? Well, look around you. Look at the problems we experience today. Depression is a common illness worldwide, with an estimated 3.8% of the population affected, including 5.0% among adults. At its worst, depression can lead to suicide. Current stats reveal that over 700,000 people die due to suicide every year. After experiencing all of this, I realized that I would be a hypocrite if I sat back and did nothing about it. In *Battling to Breathe*, I share three key tips for any human to become better than they are now.

The first tip is to learn how to GROW through the pain rather than just going through it. The second one is learning to find your purpose in your pain. And the third is to turn your pain into a success story, and using the knowledge you gained to contribute to the world. The course is available on Udemy, search for Battling to Breath. I think it will really inspire you. Finally, turning your Pain into a success story and Contributing to the World. If you would like to learn more, gp onto Udemy and search for Battling to Breathe. I have no doubt that you will love this seven-day course.

Final Words

My friends, I would like to leave you with this message:

Humans of today need to realize that "It is okay, not to be okay." Gone are the days where we think that we can solve every problem that we face. Our conditioned backgrounds taught us that we are not allowed to show emotions, we should be this rock that everyone looks up to, but that is all changing. Now we are able to tap into our true emotions and heal ourselves, so we can truly be the people we are meant to be. Remember, loving yourself is not selfish in this century. My last words are, when we fix our inner world, our family, partner, and work relationships automatically work out better.

About the Author

Nolan Pillay is a Human Mindset Specialist, a Life Coach, Inspirational and Motivational Speaker, Enlightened Warrior, and Author of the book *My COVID Journey*. He is also the brilliant and dynamic founder of the trademarked self-development programme: *Be the BEST Version of YOURSELF*™ running under the company StraightTalkWithNolan (Pty) Ltd.

His latest online course called *Battling to Breathe* speaks about mental wellness, depression, suicide, limiting beliefs, and how we as humans go through life allowing ourselves to feel suffocated. It details the steps you can take to change your life.

Nolan is also a philanthropist who uses his foundation Be the BEST version of YOURSELF to help those in need. Each year, his foundation works on various projects. This year they will climb one of the highest mountains in Africa, Mt Kilimanjaro to raise funds and give the gift of hearing to a child. Even more inspiring is that five of the seven climbers are from the deaf community.

Nolan believes this is the start to bridge the gap between the hearing community and the deaf community.

Author's Contact Information

Email: nolan@straighttalkwithnolan.com
Website: https://nolanpillay360.com/

Total Financial Transformation: From Negative Net Worth to Financial Freedom at 40

by Diego Taira

If you don't come from a rich family, a rich family must come from you.

~Diego Taira

was born in Buenos Aires, Argentina, which is a third world country economically. My parents were incredibly hard working entrepreneurs who always put their kids first. Although we were not wealthy, my parents made sure that we never lacked anything that was necessary. I was raised in an environment of frugality and hard work, and I learned the values of dedication and perseverance from my parents.

When I was 14 years old, my mother passed away from 'Karoshi', a Japanese term used to describe the condition of overworking. It was a huge shock for me and my siblings, and it left us with financial difficulties. My father decided to move our family back to Japan where we had to sell all of our assets just to sustain ourselves. We soon realized that we had only enough money to survive for a few months in a country where everything was so expensive. My father was forced to leave us behind and work far away to support us. It was a difficult time, but, with my two elder sisters, we managed to make it through the next four years. I spent my teens year without my parent's support or love. The need to make money was the highest priority to survive.

When I turned 18, my father became very ill and underwent two major operations. He almost died and we were amazed when he had a miraculous recovery. This was another event that has stuck with me, because it was a reminder that life is precious and we should do our best to make the most of it. The Universe had given our family a second chance. We all moved and lived together for the next couple of years.

I knew that I didn't want to fall into the same trap as my mother and father, where they worked so hard to survive that it cost them their health and our happiness. As my parents could not even complete high school, I decided to go to a university, get a good job in a great company, earn a lot of money, and become wealthy. I knew that I needed to work to earn the money to pay for my university fees as my father could not afford it. I worked my ass off to pay for the classes while my friends were partying most of the week.

I was determined to learn everything I could about proper money management and making my money work harder for me and not me for the money. I needed to learn how to invest and let it compound. I started on my financial transformational journey even though I had a negative net worth due to my education loans. I worked hard and saved enough money to alleviate my stress and invest in the stock market. At first, my investment portfolio grew steadily, but then my portfolio dipped.

Around 2006, I experienced another financial crisis when my sister came to me with a lot of debt. I had no other choice but to help her out financially, and it took a toll on my own savings. After 20-plus years, I haven't collected it back yet.

Right after that, the 2008 financial crisis hit me really hard. My entire portfolio dropped by 50%. It was an emotional rollercoaster, and hard to handle. I never gave up, though, I continued on my quest to become financially free. I continued to learn about different asset classes from books and I even attended paid courses. I knew that I needed to take decisive action, and believe in the process until I finally succeeded.

Over the course of the second decade of my investing, I exponentially grew my knowledge, my experience, and emotional control ability. These were all crucial factors in achieving financial success. Investing in the stock market requires a strong character of self-discipline, resilience, courage, and patience. Working hard and smart is also necessary to achieve exponential results which pay off.

I have continually searched for greater options that could outperform the market, grow my portfolio, and achieve my financial goals earlier. After two decades of studying the fundamentals of businesses, from dividend machines to asset-heavy companies, from growth stocks to hyper-grow businesses to options tradings. I can proudly say that I mastered the science and art of stock investing.

After working for 18 years in an MNC company, at the age of 40, I embraced the FIRE mentality (Financial Independence, Retire Early or Retire Enablement) and fired my bosses so that I could become the CEO of my life.

It wasn't easy, but it was worth it. The path to financial freedom is well-known, but it's not often traveled. I want to give you this encouragement right from the start, if I was able to do it, you can do it too.

Being in the market and learning the hard way was not easy and certainly, it was a lonely journey that might scare off many people. I knew that once the information was learned, though, that anyone could achieve financial independence and I was super motivated to help others accomplish what I had. I decided to create a community called "Wealth

Angels", where we are teaching all about personal finances, and investing. It's a wonderful community where we are teaching all those things that formal education, our parents, or society never taught us. We are helping each other to reach financial freedom together.

My mission is to help others achieve financial freedom so they can focus on what matters to them in life. I strongly believe that financial freedom is just the starting point. Once you have achieved it, you can live your purpose in life and give more of your gifts to the world. You can leave a legacy and bless the next generations to come. This is the ripple effect that I hope we will create together.

We can inspire, impact, and transform individuals' financial lives so they can live an extraordinary and abundant lifestyle. Starting with our kids, closest family members, and then the whole world. If your life's vision is to make an impact on your loved ones and the people around you, a financial mindset shift is something you might need to deal with first. Don't let it be left up to destiny; make your own destiny, and live an extraordinary life.

I hope that my transformational story helps you get inspired to make your own story and reach financial freedom with others. Together, we can create a better world for ourselves and our loved ones.

I've become financially free at the age of 40. This is the basic framework that I used.

The Three Steps to Reach Financial Success

Step #1. Bring awareness of your current situation and your destination

Once you are aware of your current financial situation and where you want to go, you can create a financial plan & strategy to help you reach your destination.

A : Know your current situation by knowing your current cash flow

1. *Active Income* refers to the money you earn through your personal efforts, such as working a job or running a business.
2. *Passive Income* refers to the income that you earn through interest, dividends, rental income, royalties, or other sources that generate income without requiring ongoing effort from you.
3. *Capital Gain Income* refers to the profit you earn from the sale of a capital asset, such as stocks, real estate, or artwork.

1. Active Income	2. Passive Income	3. Capital Gain Income	4. Other income	5.Total Income

If you are 100% dependent on your *active income* from your employer or business, you still have a long way to go.

B : Know where you want to go by knowing your Financial Freedom Number

The Financial Freedom Number refers to the amount of money you need to have saved or invested in order to achieve financial freedom. It means that you have enough passive income or capital gain income from your investments to cover your living expenses without having to work for money. Or, work because you want and not because you need to.

The Financial Freedom Number varies from person to person, as it depends on factors such as your lifestyle, expenses, and retirement goals. To calculate your Financial Freedom Number, you would typically start by determining your annual expenses, subtracting any passive income you currently have, and multiplying the remaining amount by the number of years you plan to be financially independent.

Financial Freedom Number: Is your desired monthly expenses after retirement x12

	Financial Freedom Number	Total Annual Income	GAP	GAP %

GAP Number : Financial Freedom Number – (Total Annual Income – Active Income)

*Unless you would like to continue doing a part-time job or full time job as you love what you do, deduct or reduce the active income from the Total Annual Income.

You need Step #2. in order to reduce your GAP % over the years.

Step #2. Build your plan, goals, and strategy to make it happen

Financial freedom can be defined as the ability to live comfortably without worrying about money. This can be achieved through a combination of smart financial planning, disciplined saving, and strategic investment. Here are some plans, goals, and strategies that can help you achieve financial freedom:

Create your simple money management system

One of the most popular money management systems is the **"T Harv Eker's 6 Jar System"**.

The 6 Jar System involves dividing your income into six different "jars" based on a specific percentage of your income. The jars are as follows:

1. *Necessities (55%):* This jar is for your essential expenses, such as rent/mortgage, utilities, food, and transportation.
2. *Long-term Savings* (10%): This jar is for long-term savings goals, such as down payment on a house or kid's education.

3. *Education* (10%): This jar is for personal and professional development, such as courses, workshops, and books.
4. *Play* (10%): This jar is for discretionary spending, such as entertainment, hobbies, and vacations.
5. Give (5%): This jar is for charitable giving or acts of kindness, such as donating to a charity or helping a friend in need.
6. *Financial Freedom* (10%): This jar is for building wealth and creating passive and active income streams.

Here are the steps :

- Determine your income: Calculate your total monthly income, including your salary, side hustle income, and any other sources of revenue.
- Allocate your income: Based on the T Harv Eker 6 Jar System, allocate a specific percentage of your income to each jar.
- Automate your allocations: Set up automatic transfers to each jar to ensure that you're consistently allocating your income according to your plan. This will also help you avoid overspending in any one category.
- Review and adjust regularly: Review your allocations and expenses regularly to make sure you're on track to reach your financial goals. Adjust your allocations as needed to account for unexpected expenses or changes in income. Increase your Financial Freedom jar whenever possible.

By following these steps, you can create a simple money management system based on the *T Harv Eker 6 Jar System* that helps you manage your money effectively, build wealth, and achieve financial freedom.

Strategy to Achieve Financial Freedom

Prepare your budget and cut unnecessary costs

Direct your money based on your spending plan (a.k.a budget). Spend gratefully on things and experiences that bring you joy. Cut unnecessary expenses that do not, and live below your means.

Pay Yourself First

Prioritize your own financial goals before anything else by setting aside the % mentioned above for the Financial Freedom jar before you pay your bills or spend money on discretionary expenses. This will set yourself to success in the long run.

Build your emergency funds

Knowing that you have a financial safety net in case of an emergency can provide peace of mind and reduce stress. This can also help you focus on your long-term financial goals. Aim to save at least three to six months of living expenses in an easily accessible savings account.

Protect Against Life's Uncertainty

Life is unpredictable, and it's impossible to predict what might happen in the future. Everyone has to protect themself and their family against life's uncertainties. *Insurance* is a critical tool for protecting against life's uncertainties. Consider purchasing health insurance, life insurance, disability insurance, and other types of insurance as appropriate. These policies can help protect you and your family financially in case of unexpected events such as illness, injury, or death.

Emergency Fund: Building an emergency fund can provide a cushion to help you weather unexpected financial setbacks. Aim to save at least three to six months of living expenses in an easily accessible savings account.

Estate Planning: Estate planning is the process of preparing for the management and distribution of your assets after your death. Consider creating a will, a trust, and other estate planning documents to ensure that your wishes are carried out and your assets are distributed according to your wishes.

Attack your debt

Make a list of all your debts: Make a list of all your debts, including the balance, interest rate, and minimum monthly payment. This will help you prioritize which debts to tackle first. Here are the top two strategies you can use to attack your debt:

Snowball method: With the snowball method, you pay off your debts in order of smallest to largest balance, regardless of interest rate. Once you pay off the smallest debt, you move on to the next smallest debt, and so on. This method can be motivating because you see progress quickly.

Avalanche method: With the avalanche method, you pay off your debts in order of highest to lowest interest rate. This method saves you the most money on interest over time, but may take longer to see progress.

By attacking your debt with a clear strategy and dedication, you can take control of your finances and make your money work harder for you.

Increase the wage between your income and expenses

Increase your income: Look for ways to increase your income, such as negotiating a raise at work, taking on a side hustle, or starting your own business. Increasing your income will help you widen the gap between your income and expenses, giving you more money to save and invest.

Invest in an asset class that will grow your wealth

This is one of the most important parts of the process. Develop a long-term investment strategy that aligns with your financial goals and risk tolerance. Consider investing in a diversified portfolio of stocks, real estate, or business to help grow your wealth and let it compound over time.

Monitor and adjust your plan

Regularly monitor your progress towards your financial goals and adjust your plan as needed. Stay committed to your plan, and make changes when necessary to stay on track towards financial freedom.

The above steps are well-known but not well traveled. Every single person who did reach financial freedom has certainly applied these steps. I am sure you can do it too.

Remember to stay disciplined, track your progress, and adjust your plan as needed.

Step #3. Create your own supporting board members

Having your financial freedom board member makes the difference.

Having a support system can be incredibly helpful in achieving financial freedom. This support system could include family, friends, a wealth coach, a mentor, or a like minded community. Here are a few ways that having a support system can help:

Accountability: When you have people who are invested in your financial success, you're more likely to stay on track and achieve your goals. This can be particularly helpful if you tend to procrastinate or struggle with self-discipline.

Knowledge and expertise: Financial advisors and mentors can provide valuable knowledge and expertise that you may not have. They can offer advice, answer questions, and help you make informed decisions about your finances.

Encouragement: Achieving financial freedom can be a long and challenging journey. Having people in your corner who believe in you and encourage you can help keep you motivated and focused on your goals.

Emotional support: Financial stress can take a toll on your mental and emotional well-being. Having a support system that you can turn to for emotional support can be incredibly helpful.

Networking opportunities: Building a network of like-minded individuals who are also pursuing financial freedom can provide opportunities for learning, growth, and collaboration.

Overall, having a support system can be a valuable asset in achieving financial freedom. They can provide accountability, knowledge, encouragement, emotional support, and networking opportunities, all of which can help you stay on track and achieve your financial goals.

If you really want to dive deep into these three steps, you could claim access to the FREE ebook from here. www.wealth-angels.com/resources/ FFF-ebook (Soon to be updated)

If you want to learn how to invest in the stock market in order to grow your wealth exponentially, check the Wealth Angels website.

If you are born poor, it's not your mistake,
But if you die poor, it is your mistake.
~Bill Gates

Author Contact Information

Email: diego@wealth-angels.com
Website: www.wealth-angels.com
LinkedIn: https://www.linkedin.com/in/diegotaira/
Instagram: https://www.instagram.com/diegotaira_archangel/

If you don't like something, change it.
If you can't change it, change your attitude."

~Maya Angelou

Release, Reframe and Rebirth

by Andreea Tamas

I can be changed by what happens to me.
But I refuse to be reduced by it.

~Maya Angelou

s I slowly opened my eyes, I felt a sharp pain in my left arm. I tried to move, but my body felt heavy and weak, like I had been asleep for a long time. I looked down and saw a thin plastic tube inserted into my vein, connected to a bag of clear liquid, hanging on a metal stand beside my bed. Looking around the room, I felt a sense of disorientation and confusion. It was a small, dimly lit space with white walls and a single window covered with blinds. Panic set in as I realized no one was in the room with me. I felt alone and scared, unable to remember anything from the past few days.

I tried to speak, but my throat felt dry and sore, and my voice came out as a faint whisper. My mind raced with questions. Had I been in an accident? Was I in a hospital? How long had I been unconscious? Are all my body parts intact? The uncertainty of my situation only made me feel more anxious and helpless. Tears streamed down my face as I lay there, trying to understand everything. I longed for a friendly voice to tell me everything would be okay. But for now, I was alone with my thoughts, fears, and the constant beep of the monitor beside my bed. I didn't know what the future held, but for now, I was glad to be alive and hopeful that someone would soon be there to offer me comfort and answers.

Before we rewind and get into how I ended up in the hospital, let me set the intention of my chapter. We will all experience at one point in our life that moment that took us to the ground, that knockout blow. This is my story of how I got up using three tools to achieve total transformation and break out of my two-year downward spiral. Now let's return to Las Vegas in 2015, where this event occurred.

The Knockout Blow

Las Vegas, or Sin City, whatever you want to call it. For some reason, things always take a dark twist in this city. I wasn't spared from it. Three days before the hospital scene, I was with my boyfriend and another couple at a music festival we had driven to Nevada for. Despite feeling unwell that week, I ignored my body's warning signs and decided to go anyway. At twenty-five years old, safety wasn't my highest priority. In deciding to go,

I was ignoring what my body was telling me. I took some medicine, but didn't heed the instructions that warned me against mixing my medication with alcohol. As I partied into the night, my condition worsened to the point my friends said maybe I should go back to the hotel. Life-saving advice in hindsight.

I agreed to leave and my boyfriend took me back to the hotel. My fantasy plan of hydration and sleep to improve my health quickly diminished as I started throwing up. I felt so weak and helpless. Blurred memories of my boyfriend helping me were all I recall. My condition worsened as I collapsed to the floor and started having a seizure and choking. My boyfriend called the ambulance and provided me with mouth-to-mouth resuscitation while waiting. All of this is information fed to me afterwards, as my memory of the events is infinitesimal.

Fast forward past the ambulance ride, through the allergy testing and all of the doctor's procedures. I barely remember any of it and eventually, I slipped into a coma. I woke up in a white hospital robe and had no idea of anything for the last two and a half days. My last memory was feeling unwell at the music festival.

My boyfriend came and explained to me what had happened. As he continued speaking, my thoughts drifted, "How can this happen to me?" A sense of contraction, shame, and anger gripped me from within as I got pissed that I mixed medication and alcohol. Then my boyfriend dropped a comment that shook my world. He said, "The doctors don't know when the next seizure will happen or how it's triggered. You need to use extreme caution going forth."

Wait, what? What was going on? I thought it was a simple incident of mixing medication with alcohol but it's more than that? Now I have to live in constant fear that this might happen again? I was shaken to my core.

I finally got discharged from the hospital, and we spent another night in Vegas before heading back to Lake Tahoe. The drive back was long, but I slept most of the way. I was rattled at how my life had just turned upside down.

The next few weeks were absolute hell. I had frequent headaches on top of the anxiety related to the fact that I might have another seizure. I was extra careful with everything, eliminating alcohol from my diet and focusing on making wise decisions that best served my mind and body. I started to feel better and things felt calmer. I thought I was on the mend until the doors to hell fully opened.

You see, I started to realize that I had side effects from the episode in Vegas. I was shocked to discover I had minor memory loss. Several memories and experiences from my twenty-five years on this planet had vanished. My boyfriend had to remind me of places we had already been, people we had met, and experiences we had shared. Being in an accident was one thing, but losing some memories made me feel incomplete, scared, and helpless.

The final knockout blow came a few weeks later. I thought that dealing with this issue was tough, but the hits kept coming. One day, I opened the mail one day and was stunned to find a bill from the hospital. It turns out that being uninsured in the United States of America and spending three days in a hospital meant a huge five-figure bill. I dropped the paper as I read the amount. In a sudden swift rush of emotion, I realized I totally hated my life. I was overwhelmed, stressed, and anxious at all the calamity that had befallen me.

Between 2015 and 2017, hate, anger, frustration, self-shaming, self-sabotage, and madness became underlying emotional themes in my life. I currently avoid such negative words in my vocabulary, but this was my reality eight years ago. When you feel broken, not normal, and incomplete, dealing with mild amnesia and financial debt, madness and chaos can become a fixed fixture in life. It happened to me, and it happens more often than we are aware of.

The good news in between all the falling parts was that I had a payment plan with the hospital's financial division. The bad news is I had to work fourteen to fifteen-hour days, six to seven days a week, to pay off my debt. I was working two jobs and had no life. The life that I did have in between work was anchored in anger and negative self-talk. I was struggling.

The only place I felt relief was at the gym. The gym was one of my channels to take out the frustration I felt about the state of my life. In hindsight, I am super grateful that I had that. As I threw myself into working out, I started to feel better. The headaches became less frequent over the years after the incident, but I was in a dark place, unable to see the light at the end of the tunnel. I was on the fast track to burnout.

Rising from the Ashes

As a child, I grew up with an over-achieving brother who made great results look effortless. I, on the other hand, had to work super hard to reach above-average results. That self-generated comparison with my brother would always drive my ambition to do more and be more. This was my superpower. During my dark period of being a depressed workaholic, my inner child's ambitious superpower started asking me to strive for more than just my current predicament.

The double-edged sword of long working hours and the financial rewards allowed me to pay the hospital bill. Better yet, I even saved money due to a non-existing social life. Late in 2017, the light within me began to shine again, projecting hope. As I began to feel better, I realized that everything in life is temporary, from our time on this planet to our experiences. This thought triggered me to acquire a perspective change, asking what is possible with my life. I was able to bring myself out of a very difficult place, and I want to share what I have learned with you so that if you ever find yourself in a tough spot, you can use this technique.

My Perspective Change

Here are some of my most significant perspective changes that helped me to release the negative emotions within:

- I chose to forgive myself for having the seizure in Vegas, and release the way I was holding the story that was not serving me.
- Till now, I was angry at the doctors and the hospital bill. I reframed the situation to thank the doctors for saving my life.
- I was grateful to be alive and have a second chance at life.
- I will learn to love myself again! Love brings out my best, so I will operate in this domain.

- Having a second chance meant more opportunities.
- I could now set a life purpose that helps me understand why I am here on this planet.

My breakthrough transformational moment was planting seeds of hope, faith, gratefulness, and love. I would love to say this happened overnight, but it took a few months. While the three tools I will reveal will be more step-by-step processes, four things are imperative to transformational change that I have learnt in my journey. These are forgiveness, gratitude, purpose, and authenticity.

Four Tools for Transformational Change

Forgiveness

Forgiveness is a powerful and transformative act that can heal wounds, restore relationships, and bring peace to our lives. It is an act that starts with self-forgiveness, which is the most challenging but most important step before you can forgive others. Learning how to forgive allowed me to release my hurt, anger, and resentment towards myself and others. It helped me choose to move forward with compassion and understanding.

When we forgive, we release ourselves from the emotional pain and suffering that comes along with holding onto grudges and resentments. We free ourselves from the negative energy that keeps us stuck in the past and prevents us from living fully in the present. Moreover, forgiveness has the power to repair and even strengthen relationships. It allows us to see the humanity in others and empathize with their struggles and challenges. When we forgive others, we open up reconciliation and growth possibilities.

Forgiveness is a gift we give ourselves and others. It allows us to move forward with grace, compassion, and love. By practicing forgiveness, we can create a more peaceful and harmonious world, one relationship at a time. The best part is that forgiveness allows us to truly nurture our own relationship with ourselves.

Gratitude

Gratitude is a powerful tool that transformed my life in numerous ways. Using gratitude, I began to feel grateful for my past and for what I already have. It shifted my focus from what I lacked to what I had.

The power of gratitude is immense. Instead of dwelling on the negative aspects of our lives, we can train our minds to see the positive and be thankful for the blessings that come our way. This shift in perspective can lead to greater happiness, contentment, and inner peace. When we cultivate a sense of gratitude, we can appreciate the abundance and beauty surrounding us, even in difficult times.

Another benefit of practicing gratitude is that we can improve our relationships with others. When we express gratitude towards those who have helped or shown us kindness, we strengthen our connections with them and deepen our sense of community. The power of gratitude lies in its ability to bring joy and contentment into our lives and strengthen our relationships with others. By practicing gratitude daily, I cultivated a positive mindset that allowed me to live more fully and appreciate the world. It worked for me and it can work for you too.

Purpose

Instilling a sense of purpose was essential for me on my quest to live a fulfilling and meaningful life. Purpose gives me direction, motivation, and a sense of identity. It drove me to get up daily and pursue my goals and aspirations. Before my breakthrough, I aimed to pay my bills and hoped my life would improve. Purpose allowed me to get more clarity on what I desired long term, not from one project to the next. It also allowed me to get to know myself, who I am, what I want, what I desire, what my needs are, and how I can make myself happy from the inside out. It helped me to escape the trap of constantly searching outside myself for happiness, either in a job, making more money, moving to a new place, or with my partner.

Instilling purpose allowed me to ask questions about life, like:

- What are all my life projects leading up to?

163

- What is the big end game?
- What is my definition of happiness?
- What is it that I truly desire and need?

The power of purpose lies in its ability to provide a sense of meaning and significance in our lives. When we have a clear purpose, we can focus our energies and efforts towards achieving our goals. This can lead to a greater sense of accomplishment and satisfaction in life. Purpose can also give us a sense of belonging and community. When we have a shared purpose with others, we can form deeper connections and work towards a common goal. This can lead to greater unity, cooperation, and a greater sense of contribution to something larger than ourselves.

Purpose can give us a sense of resilience and perseverance in facing challenges and adversity. When we have a strong sense of purpose, we can better overcome obstacles and stay committed to our goals despite setbacks and failures.

The power of purpose lies in its ability to provide us with direction, motivation, meaning, and resilience in life. By cultivating a strong sense of purpose, we can begin living a more fulfilling and purposeful life, and that means we can contribute to the world in a much more meaningful way.

Authenticity

I used to hide my feelings. I would always show up with a smile on my face. I spent a lot of time pretending all was well. That was my former self. During my tough times, lying through a smile and convincing people I had my shit together felt like the right thing to do. It created a lot of distance between me and other people, and I often felt insincere and disconnected from others. When I finally started sharing my feelings honestly with others, a whole new world opened up to me.

Authenticity is a powerful force that transformed my life in profound ways. It meant being true to myself and my values and aligning with my deep beliefs and desires. When I chose to be authentic, I got to live with integrity and be true to myself, leading to greater self-acceptance and self-esteem. The power of authenticity activated my ability to bring greater meaning, purpose, and fulfillment into my life.

Authenticity taps into the truth of who you really are. Being vulnerable allows you to connect authentically with others. The solution to your issues might be with the person you speak to, but if you never speak the truth, then that opportunity vanishes. Moreover, authenticity can deepen our connections with others. When we are authentic, we can form more profound, deeper meaningful relationships with others, showing up as our true selves and connecting with others on a deeper level.

Another great benefit of authenticity is that it can lead to greater creativity and innovation. When we are authentic, we can tap into our unique perspectives and insights, leading to new and innovative ideas and approaches. The power of authenticity lies in its ability to bring greater meaning, purpose, and fulfillment into our lives, deepen our connections with others, and fuel creativity and innovation. By embracing our true selves and living in alignment with our values and beliefs, we can live a more authentic and fulfilling life.

I have never looked back once I chose to be authentic in my identity. I now have deeper friendships and I feel safe now, able to share all of my feelings. Not just the good feelings but all of them… the great, the beautiful, the bad, and the more negative feelings. People respond to me totally differently now that I am showing my true self, and finally I am attracting the kind of people into my life who are aligned with who I really am. Try it, it might just change your life.

Techniques for Transformation

I'm fortunate and grateful to share these tools to save you time on your transformational healing journey. In order to really bring these tools to life, I have created some easy techniques you can use for transformation. The techniques listed below are built on forgiveness, gratefulness, authenticity, and purpose.

Tool One: Release

If you have been alive for a decade or two, it is possible that there are some emotions deep within you that are hindering your progress in life. You may not be consciously aware of these stuck emotions on a daily basis, but they are clogging you up and robbing you of precious emotional bandwidth that could be used for more joy, lightness, and bliss.

I learned this profound exercise from one of my favorite people, Lisa Nichols, who inspired me to share my voice on a larger scale. This mirror exercise has been beneficial for me in releasing various emotions such as guilt, shame, and others.

The Thirty-Day Mirror Exercise Challenge

I encourage you to practice this exercise daily for at least 30 days. Simply choose a sacred space where you can't be disturbed. Ensure you feel safe and have a mirror. Dedicate at least five minutes to this exercise. Staring into your eyes in the mirror:

- *"(Say your name); I'm proud that you (and state seven things you're proud of)."*
- *"(Say your name); I forgive you for (and state seven things you forgive yourself for)."*
- *"(Say your name); I commit you to that (and state seven commitments)."*

Embrace and Release Your Emotions

Embrace any emotions that may come up while doing the mirror exercise. You may feel the need to cry, and this is normal. Just let yourself go with the flow and release old beliefs and ways of being. It is imperative not to judge yourself or your emotions in this process. You can also hug yourself and use comforting words such as: 'I'm here for you', 'I love you', and 'I understand'.

Once you are done releasing, answer these questions:

1. *What is present for you now?*

2. *How did it feel to really feel that emotion?*
3. *What did you learn from expressing that emotion?*

Acknowledge Your Growth

I recommend having a journal where you write about your experience during this process, so you can witness your breakthroughs and see the gradual and powerful transformation happening for you.

Tool Two: Reframe How You Look at Things

Reframing a situation allows you to see it from another perspective. The meaning of any event depends on the frame in which we perceive it. By giving yourself the flexibility to change how you see something, you can achieve your outcomes more efficiently.

Reframing changes the way you feel and, therefore, what you do. I want to invite you to ask yourself these two questions to help you reframe your past experiences so you feel empowered about them instead of being the victim:

1. *What else could this mean?*
2. *What's the cost of continuing to believe this?*
3. *What is good about this?*

You cannot go back and change the facts, but you can change how you hold into those facts.

Tool Three: Rebirth

Think about the answer to this question: "What is that new identity you want to embody?"

Identity is created through experiences, interpretations, and beliefs.

The first thing you want to become evident in this step is, what is your identity right now? To find out, answer these questions:

- *What are the patterns of my life? (any pattern is a reflection of your identity)*
- *What are my gifts?*
- *Who can I trust?*
- *Will I be wealthy?*

Your self-image/identity *controls* your life. Everything you *do* or *do not do* is an identity reflection. It is usually easy to do what you are and hard to do what you are not.

The "Act as If" Exercise

This is a handy frame to help you realize what it would be like if you achieved your outcome and got yourself out of a stuck state. This gets you to associate with that outcome, and by doing so, you create that as a possibility.

Question:

Imagine if you had achieved X goal entirely in the best possible way. *What would you see, hear, feel, and say to yourself which would confirm that you'd already succeeded?*

By taking yourself in the future and answering the above question, you are already rehearsing a possible future. Your mind does not know the difference between reality and your manifested imaginative construct.

Final Words

It Doesn't Matter Who You Are Today.
It Only Matters Who You Want to Become.
And the Price You're Willing to Pay to Get There.
~Tom Bilyeu

This quote was the beginning of my transformation. The moment I read this quote, I realized for the first time that I have the power within myself to change who I was, who I am, and who I want to become. Let it have a similar effect on you on your journey. Imagine who you want to become, and then roll up your sleeves and get to work creating that future version of yourself.

About the Author

Andreea is in love with life and people. She is a certified Coach, Speaker, and Trainer with John Maxwell, a Reiki Practitioner, and a Sacred Transitions specializing in Akashic Records.

After moving from Romania to the USA in 2014, she worked in management consulting. In 2019, she began to feel frustrated and overwhelmed in the corporate world, and she decided to make a change. She shifted her focus to concentrate on her coaching business, because she recognized that coaching was in true alignment with her most divine path.

Her mission is to take you through the most needed and sacred transition, moving from scarcity, overthinking, and brain fatigue into the connection with your higher self, from which your unique legacy can fully blossom and build a life by design. Andreea guides people experiencing change, whether they want to move to a new country or place, change their job, start their business or go through a loss. She helps you activate your power and rewire your brain so you can show up in your life with confidence and certainty.

Author Contact Information

Email: andreeatamascoaching@gmail.com
Website: https://www.instagram.com/asacred_rebel

Life keeps throwing me stones.
And I keep finding the diamonds.

~Ana Claudia Antunes

Embracing Adversity: A Journey from Ordinary to Extraordinary

by Lawrence Tuazon

Life's journey may lead us to the depths of rock bottom, but it is in those dark moments that we discover the strength to rise, rebuild, and embrace a life that is whole and extraordinary.

~Lawrence Tuazon

As you are reading this book, my heart overflows with gratitude and purpose. Looking back at my journey, I am humbled by the transformation life has gifted me. From an ordinary life filled with struggles to an extraordinary path of empowerment, I have learned that every challenge carries the potential for greatness.

The Struggle to Succeed and Climbing the Corporate Ladder

I was born and raised in the Philippines, I pursued my dreams with determination and diligence. My early life was a struggle and my mom worked overseas to provide for us, and her unwavering strength became my inspiration. I believed that hard work and sacrifice were the key to a better life. I moved to Japan with dreams of success, and my Cinderella story began climbing the ladder in my first full time job in a giant retail company. I was driven by the belief that success required sacrifices, and so I poured all my time and effort into being number one in every job that I had. Moving from department to department, I had one goal and that was to be the best.

Yes, I became number one.

Yes, I got the recognition and promotion that I desired.

But the price was steep. I had failed at taking care of the most important thing in me. I had failed my body; I failed my health.

Success was all I sought, and the more career success I had, the more I worked.

I remember after I got married to my wife. I became part of the core management team, and I began to work between 13 and 15 hours per day. I was eating convenience store food at work because I was always on the go. I slept for five hours per night, and I did that for a full five years.

Yes, five hours per night of sleep for five long years. And I thought that this was a normal thing because my colleagues were doing the very same thing. We were working under high pressure to achieve target sales plans and goals. We were overworked and totally stressed out. I thought I was invincible, that the price of success was worth the sacrifice. I sacrificed my health, my sleep, and my happiness in the pursuit of this elusive dream.

The High Price of Success

My wake-up call came during my annual medical checkup in 2018 when I was confronted with the reality of my deteriorating health. The doctor told me to come back again to repeat a part of the check up and redo my blood test because of the alarming result. I was so shocked.

After the checkup, I knew I was harming myself, I knew I had to get healthy, but I simply didn't know how I could do that. I couldn't quit my job because that was the only way I had to provide for my family. For my wonderful wife and my brand-new baby daughter. I had to work to give us a better life and a brighter future. I decided to ignore my health and just keep working. I believed this was the right thing to do, Success equals sacrifice but I was very wrong.

In addition to harming my health, I was also harming my relationship with my wife. We had a brand-new baby to take care of but I was never home. My wife needed me to help her, but I was always working overtime. By the time I came home each night I was drained and tired and all I could do was eat and go to sleep. I lived in this cycle for years. Maybe you can relate? Many of us have been on this hamster wheel.

The Tragic Accident and Refusing Defeat

One fateful day in September 2018, life dealt me a crushing blow that shattered my reality. I had an accident at work. A forklift crushed my right leg. I don't remember much but I do remember the extreme pain I was in. It was all blurry and I was rushed to the hospital. Everything was getting dark. I was sure that I was going to die. It was so terrifying. I lost 4 liters of blood and was unconscious for three days. When I woke up, I was in the ICU. My wife is crying. When she saw me open my eyes she ran over and hugged me. I'll never forget her words. She said, "I'm so glad that you're awake now and still with us. Please hold on! I love you and we need you!" I cried. And then, I noticed my leg. It was still there but it looked horrifically damaged.

The doctor stepped into the room. He told me how badly damaged my leg was and my best chance for me to survive would be if I amputated my leg.

My mind flinched when I heard this. Amputate my leg? No! Never! I did not want to lose my leg and I would not lose it.

I was terrified. And so, I refused my doctor's order. And for the next six months I fought for my leg. I did anything and everything I could do. I underwent ten major surgeries including skin grafting and muscle transplants in my quest to keep my leg. I even moved hospitals three times. I went above and beyond to save my leg because I simply couldn't accept the truth.

When I finally left the hospital, leaning on crutches for support, I was eager to resume my normal life. Little did I know, my leg's condition made returning to my old routine impossible.

Every day, I tried my best to walk and get back to my normal life. I remember standing at a street crossing, waiting to cross when the pedestrian light turned green. I hurriedly crossed with my injured leg, hoping to make it in time before the light changed. But it kept blinking, and I felt desperate as I tried to get to the other side. Unfortunately, the light turned red, and I was stuck in the middle of the road. The pain was unbearable, so I started taking a lot of painkillers. As winter came, my leg became even more sensitive to pain, making it harder for me to move around. I became less and less active and started eating more when I felt stressed. Before I knew it I was clinically obese, I weighed 234 pounds (106 kg).

I knew something had to change so in February of 2020, in the lowest moment of my life, I decided to remove my damaged leg. The recovery from the surgery was very difficult, I felt hopeless and helpless inside. And to escape reality, I constantly distracted myself by playing computer games and binge-watching endless television series, movies, and dramas. Social media became my constant companion, as I spent hours scrolling through other people's lives, using it as a way to divert my attention from myself, away from my own life.

After receiving my prosthetic leg, the process of learning to walk with it was excruciatingly painful. The burden of my heavy body weight made it nearly impossible for me to practice walking effectively. As a result, my muscles weakened, and I experienced atrophy due to my limited mobility.

For months, I found myself confined to my bed or a wheelchair, unable to take a single step. The inability to walk not only hindered my physical progress but also led to the loss of my job. I lost the position, fame and power that I had. All of the things that I built in my career were gone. And a deep heavy depression began to wave on me. "I'm trapped in this body, I'm trapped in this life of constant pain. Not knowing what to do with no hope inside."

Embracing Rock Bottom

I can still picture that moment so vividly – sitting in my wheelchair, watching my two-year-old daughter play in front of me. I couldn't actively participate in her joy. I couldn't lift her in my arms, walk with her hand in hand, or do the things a father should. It broke my heart as a father. It was at this moment that I started to look at myself, And realized that I needed something to change. That I had to do anything and everything I could to regain mobility for her. This was the shift I needed to make. Because what I was doing wasn't working anymore.

I had hit my rock bottom. And I was willing to let go of everything It was now or never for me, and I had to go all in.

I decided that I was ready to give myself another chance to live so that I can reach my goals and dreams in life. I'm ready!

The Miraculous Shift in Perception

I embarked on a journey of self-discovery, learning how to embrace life as an amputee. It hit me that my disability didn't have to hold me back; it was just a part of who I am. Instead of counting on what I lost, I started focusing on what I still had – a resilient body and a determined mind. And every day, I chose to bless and appreciate my strengths rather than cursing my weaknesses. I accepted that what's gone is gone.

In the midst of this transformation, I asked myself, "What do I still have?" The answer was clear – my family. Throughout my challenging journey, my incredible wife and precious daughter stood by me, offering unwavering love and support. Their love became my driving force, and I knew I couldn't give up. They were there for me when I needed them the most and now, I wanted to be there for them. I knew they are waiting for me. And I began to heal inside and out.

The Extraordinary Tool: Radical Acceptance and a Growth Mindset Tool

I used this tool in starting my life again that led me to the sustainable mind shift that I needed, altering the way I viewed life's challenges and situations with acceptance and surrender to the process, I found newfound strength and magic seemed to follow my commitment to self-improvement.

1. Embrace Radical Acceptance: The first step is to accept your current circumstances, no matter how challenging they may be. Recognize that life may not always go as planned, and that's okay. Avoid resisting or denying your reality. Instead, acknowledge it and understand that it's a part of your journey. Embrace your experiences, whether positive or negative, and use them as stepping stones for growth.

2. Release Blame and Self-Judgment: Let go of any blame you place on yourself or others for your current situation. Self-judgment will only hold you back from moving forward. Understand that it's okay to make mistakes; they are opportunities for learning and improvement. Forgive yourself and others, and free yourself from the burden of guilt.

3. Cultivate a Growth Mindset: Embrace the belief that your abilities and intelligence can be developed through dedication and hard work. See challenges and setbacks as opportunities for learning and growth, not as indicators of failure. Embrace the process

of learning and improving, rather than fixating on immediate outcomes.

4. Be Open to Change and New Possibilities: Stay open-minded and be willing to explore new opportunities and perspectives. Embrace change as a chance for growth and development. Be adaptable in the face of challenges and see them as opportunities to evolve and become stronger.

5. Set Inspiring Goals: Create a vision for your extraordinary life. Set inspiring and achievable goals that align with your passions and values. Break them down into smaller, actionable steps to keep yourself motivated and on track.

6. Take Inspired Action: Act upon your goals with determination and enthusiasm. Draw upon your newfound strength and resilience to take bold steps towards your dreams. Embrace the journey, knowing that every step, no matter how small, brings you closer to living an extraordinary life.

7. Seek Support and Community: Surround yourself with like-minded individuals who support and uplift you. Connect with a community that encourages personal growth and development. Share your experiences, learn from others, and offer support in return.

8. Practice Gratitude: Cultivate a mindset of gratitude for what you have, even amidst challenges. Gratitude opens the door to a positive perspective and helps you focus on the abundance in your life. Celebrate your progress, no matter how small, and appreciate the journey towards your extraordinary life.

By incorporating Radical Acceptance and a Growth Mindset into your life, you can break free from the shackles of self-limiting beliefs and move towards an extraordinary existence. Embrace the power within you to transform challenges into opportunities and embark on a journey of growth and personal fulfillment. Remember, your extraordinary life awaits you, and you have the strength to create it.

Choosing to Live an Extraordinary Life

All the things that I wished for, and planned are now happening. To give back to the community, to help and transformed other people lives, being a Peak Performance Health and Life Coach, an Author and publisher, Being a conscious parent to my kids and a loving husband to my wife,

I regained my life.

It is not what happens to you that determines how successful and happy you are going to be. Instead, it is what you do when something happens that matters the most. It is not about the fall, but about the choices you make after you fall.

It is the thoughts that you have about the challenge that will formulate the beliefs and attitude that you have that makes the difference.

And I began to realize that I was the only one who had control over my life. I was the one who determined whether I would live and thrive or shrivel up and die, and there's no blaming allowed. It was my choice.

And I chose to live again, I chose to stand, I chose to walk and I even chose to run again. I chose to move towards the best version of myself I could possibly imagine. I chose to fly.

I'm here to tell you that you don't have to lose anything or be like me to find that greatness in you. You already have it. Trust me, you have it. It is within you and it is waiting for you. Impossibility becomes really possible when you make up your mind and Act on it.

I promise you.

You can do better than me,

Step into to that greatness in you.

I leave you with this…if I had the chance to choose between the two legged or the one legged Lawrence, I will always choose the one-legged Lawrence.

And even though I'm disabled, I'm now able to change and transform other people's lives.

My disability tells me to inspire and touch other people's lives the way I wanted to. And I will.

From the core of my heart, I appreciate your time, love and energy! Thank you very much!

Love+Strength,
Lawrence Tuazon

> *Life's challenges can be unforgiving,*
> *but within each of us lies the power to redefine what*
> *is possible and live an extraordinary life.*
> ~Lawrence Tuazon

About the Author

Lawrence Tuazon is founder of Total Health Coaching. He is an amputee who has helped and inspired thousands of people all over the world by sharing his radical health and life transformation. Lawrence is a speaker, peak performance, health and fitness coach guiding and bringing conscious permanent health and body transformation through holistic health practice. His vision is to create chronic health as the new normal instead of chronic disease and to bring holistic health education in the school curriculum.

Author Contact Information

Email: lawrencetuazon84@gmail.com
Instagram: https://instagram.com/iamlawrencetuazon?utm_
            source=qr&igshid=ZDc4ODBmNjlmNQ%3D%3D
Linkedin: https://www.linkedin.com/in/lawrence-tuazon-b32725239/

Each tiny effort builds on the next, so that brick by brick, magnificent things can be created.

~Robin Sharma

Listening at Last

by Heidi C. Tyler

The day will come when you will review your life
and be thankful for every minute of it.
Every hurt, every sorry, every joy, every celebration,
every moment of your life will be a treasure to you,
for you will see the utter perfection of the design.
You will stand back from the weaving and see the
tapestry, and you will weep at the beauty of it.

~Neale Donald Walsch

"I'm going to buy a mobility scooter, and I'm going to have the most impressive one I can find. One that people will stop and stare at and must run out of my way!" I said to my husband.

"You've got your early retirement money, so you can afford one," he replied.

"I know, but that money has got to last the rest of our lives. I'm 54 and in theory, if I live as long as mum, I've got another 20 years left. We might need that money for more important things, like the rising cost of living. Will I have the energy to even use it?" I replied.

"It's up to you dear, it's your money. Whatever you want to do is OK with me." Yes, my husband is wonderful.

The next day my husband asked me, "Did you sleep at all last night sweetheart?"

"I think I did for about 3 or 4 hours."

"Try and take a nap later. There's nothing you need to do."

"I'm so tired of it all. Every day is the same. I get up, take sixteen mega painkillers throughout the day, watch TV, get stuck inside my head, have you cook our meals, take a pill to help me sleep, get little sleep, and go over and over what has happened."

"You didn't know you were ill. It wasn't your fault. You've been incredible at reversing your diabetes since you've stopped working. That's amazing. We're going out today for a walk in the downs, do you want to come with us? We can find somewhere for you to sit and enjoy the view."

"No, I'll stay home today. I'm just too tired. Maybe next time."

I watched my family leave in the car and my mind spiraled out of control. Going over and over every scene. How my career of 36+ years came crashing down. "Needs improvement," they'd said, "bordering on inadequate." Had the years of being told I was outstanding been true? My thoughts wouldn't allow me a break, "Of course they weren't true. You're stupid."

I was in a very painful place in life. I was filled with so many doubts. I was upset that I had let myself get to be the size of a whale. Why did I do this? The answer came quickly from my overactive mind, "You have always been stupid, that's why. You didn't take care of yourself."

The weight had crept on slowly, over many years. Then I became diabetic. Just like so many of my family. I felt terrible and my thoughts swirled around. Mostly they centered around something like, "You really are stupid. You deserve this." It was a hard time for me, indeed.

How and when did I get fibromyalgia? Is it real? I sometimes wondered.

My mind would play tricks on me. I would hear myself thinking, "It's all in your head, just like that neurologist told you. You even tried to convince the doctors you had Alzheimer's or Dementia, but you haven't. You're a hypochondriac. You've always been one. You haven't got a brain that works. You never did have. That's why you were so stupid at school. Why you can never remember anything. A head full of nothing. Face facts Heidi, your teachers and dad were right all along. You're stupid and worthless. Inadequate. You've let everyone down. You are a failure."

My brain would not let up. "Yes, I am, I'm a total failure. My whole life has been a lie." No matter the topic, my brain would tell me the worst possible interpretation of my life. "You can't even manage your money well, which is why you've had to sell the family home and move here. I hope the family knows you're spending money like water. When's the financial crash going to come?"

I remember this time so clearly. Like a movie I once watched. I remember thinking that I simply did not know what to do. I knew I couldn't live like this. I prayed, "Please help me. I don't want to lay down and die. Please let there be more to my life than this."

I was searching for something, a way out of the darkness, a way out of the pain. And then, an email, from a company called Mindvalley. The ad was for a program with Jim Kwik, the foremost expert in memory improvement and brain performance. They were offering a free masterclass which promised that Jim Kwik would teach us the only skill we would ever need: Learning How to Learn.

I was intrigued. I kept listening. They said that we could rapidly clear "mental fog." That phrase struck me. It was exactly what it felt like in my head. Mental Fog. Wow. Maybe this was the answer. I decided to listen to the master class immediately, not wanting to wait a second longer. I listened and it changed my life. Honestly. It did.

I didn't fully understand how or why this had come to me right in that very moment, but however it happened was a breath of fresh air, a spark of light in my darkness. A spark that created such a monumental change in my life. I had so much fun learning the tools and techniques through this amazing course. I astounded my family with my new skills. I learned the periodic table and was able to recite it with no problem. This was huge for me, because I never even learnt that at school. I hadn't even learnt about it as a matter of fact. I had not been clever enough to be in that class.

This was exhilarating, but I could feel a part of me wanting to do more. What else could I learn? What could I learn that would help me to structure my day. I dove back into Jim Kwik. He was talking about ANT's. ANT's? Yes, but not the ones you see outside. These were automatic negative thoughts. He was saying we needed to tune into those automatic negative thoughts (ANT's) and eradicate them. This was good, now we're talking. I realized that this was just what I needed. I realized it was time to focus on me.

You see, I'd always been strong minded and strong willed at overcoming so many life challenges. I'd been incredibly resourceful. I was always looking for answers for work, for my family and friends, for anyone who needed help. I was always there for everyone else, but never for myself. I hadn't even put myself on the list. I had helped everyone with their problems and yet I hadn't looked at any of my own. Was that the reason I had accepted the slow silent death that was happening from within? Was this of my own making? How could I fix it? I was determined to figure it out.

I'd spent years telling people, "Nature has the answer." So why wasn't I looking to understand what that really meant, for me?

I was reminded again about how Jim Kwik said we should bring structure to our days. That we should examine our thoughts and eradicate the ones that were detrimental to us. I'd done these things for others but never for myself. I had done that all of my career as I sought to create a great work environment.

I realized it was time to continue to use these techniques during my retirement to heal myself. First, I had to address my weight and my diabetes. I began to learn, and eventually found a book that had been pivotal in changing my food choices, which in turn led me to finding out more. As I changed my diet, I began to lose weight and I really wanted to take the program but at the time, the approach the book was recommending was out of my financial reach. Plus, it could take years. There had to be another way.

I was told by my family that having pure oxygen in a hyperbaric chamber might be beneficial, so I researched it and found a local charity that by chance had one. It was such a new experience, and one where I got to meet other people. The majority had Multiple Sclerosis just like my dad, who died at age 66. While I was in the chamber, and on my iPad, I checked my emails..

Again, another message which was to change my life. This time, it was a program called '*Energy Medicine*' with Donna Eden. *The Energy Medicine* program is a transformational journey towards awakening your body's natural healing ability. Donna Eden had cured herself of Multiple Sclerosis!

I couldn't believe it. I wondered, "Is this for real? How is this happening? Can this really be true?" It seemed magical that this message would come to me now, as I sought to heal myself.

My excitement overflowed so much I was babbling in the chamber. I'm not sure what they thought of me right then. I didn't care though. I decided to take the plunge. I signed up as we were finishing up the treatment in the hyperbaric chamber.

Once I signed up, I couldn't wait to get started. What if it helped me? What if I could help the very people I'm with right now? I dove right in and quickly learnt the daily energy routine (DER) and did it once, twice, and even three times a day. In no time at all I could feel the shift happening in my body. The pain started declining. The energy began rising.

As each week went by, my friends in the hyperbaric chamber were commenting on how they could see me transforming. What a hilarious sight it must have been as I took them through the DER with oxygen masks over our faces. I sat in silence for the rest of the "dive" and breathed long and hard, enjoying every milliliter of oxygen I could get into my body. So clean and pure. The silence felt wonderful. A moment inside my own mind filled with joy and without the paranoia. I wanted to feel like this always.

Things were going well. And then, although it sounds too good to be true, I got another email. It seemed like my email had all the answers these days! This time for a *6 Phase Meditation with Binaural Beats* by Vishen Lakhiani. Really? Yes, I had a momentary thought wondering if the neurologist put a chip in when they took a piece of the artery in my head out to do brain tests. Oh, go on, I thought, that's crazy.

I thought about this new program and thought, "Why not?" I was ready to learn more. It was becoming a habit. The program was amazing. I learned to meditate and started a regular meditation practice. Prior to this, I'd never meditated a day in my life. Now I was totally immersed in the world of meditation.

My family was beginning to wonder about me. They worried I was getting too "Woo Woo." Was I? I thought about it, and decided that I would continue on and simply keep an open mind.

Things were going well, but then I started to have some doubts. I felt like I still had so many limitations and negative experiences and now they started to come to my mind. Ones that had contributed to my emotional instability and had spanned all 58 years of my life.

Don't get me wrong, I've had wonderful times in my life, with amazing memories, but my ever-increasing journey through meditation had opened my eyes and allowed me to see and feel more. So much weight was lifting from my mind. I thought about all the trauma of my younger years. I thought about my parents and how I had struggled to forgive them. I did eventually forgive my mum and my dad for the life I'd had from childhood. I had hated my dad for so long, and yet missed him so much when he passed. I forgave him. Even better, when I did that, I also got to forgive myself for everything I thought I'd got wrong. I had been grieving for seven years because of a mistake I made that meant I didn't get to say goodbye. I forgave myself for that. Finally!

The meditation got me to focus on things I wanted to bring into my life. I decided that I would create a vision for myself for what I wanted my life to look like in three years' time. It was tough at first. A vision? I didn't have any vision. How could I? I was stuck in this body. I didn't know of a time I had ever really had a vision for myself. I continued to think about it and slowly my vision cleared.

I knew I wanted to heal. I envisioned a life where I was completely rid of fibromyalgia and pain for good. I knew I wanted to be stronger. I started to imagine it. Could I really have such a vision? I wanted it so badly, but I could hardly breath at the thought of it, but I felt a surging passion I had never felt before. A passion for everything that lay ahead of me. I was ready to see what was next.

Slowly, I began to develop a strong belief in myself. I kept on learning amazing wellness practices like gratitude, forgiveness, and all about brules (bullshit rules). I began to create new beliefs and as I did, all my old beliefs came tumbling out. Anytime a negative thought came up, I simply reframed it. So much of me was changing. It was like I had a voice within that was getting louder and stronger. "I want to learn more, be more, grow more. I want more. I want to be free." I was helping myself, but slowly the thought became, "What if I could help others too?" This became one of my guiding forces on my healing journey. The idea that I could help others motivated me to keep going.

My life was getting better, but I knew there were still more areas of life I could address. One day, another email popped up in my inbox. Now, I know you'll be in complete disbelief, but so was I! It was another message and one I really needed to hear. When the email came in, I thought about some of the things I had learned. How we can change ourselves, our minds, and our lives when we connect with something greater than ourselves. Was this what was happening?

I thought about it and realized that I was meditating, and that had allowed me to have clarity and to sharpen my intuition. But was something more going on? Were these fortuitous messages just a coincidence, or was I really connecting to something greater? It didn't seem like these ideas could be real. Perhaps they were simply too woo woo? I didn't care. I knew they had helped me. I was listening!

The email invited me to listen to a podcast. I listened and heard all about a program called *Lifebook*. The program promised that I could become the author of my best life. I was super interested in doing the program, however, if you remember, back at the beginning of my story, I mentioned spending that was out of control. I couldn't afford the course but then, in an incredible turn of events, one of my family members gave me the money for the course. I was so grateful.

I quickly started the program and loved it from the start. It's a system where you look at twelve areas of your life and examine each one, thinking about what you want in each area. The first category is Health & Fitness, which was perfect for me. I had really come a long way in my health and I felt a sense of pride for having reversed the diabetes. As I went through the Health and Fitness category, I felt a glimmer of hope. My fibromyalgia had already become much more manageable, and the pain had become increasingly distant. I created a vision for a pain free me.

I continued the course and wondered if I could push myself even further. The next area was the Intellectual category. I thought, "No that's not me, I'll just skip through that one."

I moved onto the next section which was the Emotional category. The course gave us a week to cover this and the following category. I took a lot longer than that! As a matter of fact, I took an entire year working through those two categories. I worked through every year of my life, uncovering the stories I could remember. The stories that had created painful memories, the stories that had created so much emotional baggage. It was such a tough and draining journey. I cried so many tears and felt so many negative feelings. It was hard but I persisted. I knew it was needed so that I could let go of the past and step into my future vision. It gave me the care I needed to allow me to grow. At last, fully releasing the anger I had held onto for so long.

Once that was completed, I continued on my Lifebook journey. I got to the The Spiritual category and I skipped past it entirely. I had too much pain from having the fear of God put into me during childhood. I couldn't even address that area of my life.

I came to the Parenting category and this raised even more limiting beliefs. It took a lot to reflect on my parenting and the parenting of my own parents. This was an enlightening category for me. I learned a lot about myself and finally understood how important this category is for living a healthy life.

The Career category brought up painful memories for me. Luckily, all of the work I had done on myself had made me resilient. I felt stronger as I thought about the career I had already had and the one that I wanted to create. I continued through the categories, eventually completing all of them. Finally, I had clarity in all areas of my life.

Lifebook was a phenomenal program. They had made a lot of promises and luckily, the program delivered. It was really everything they promised it would be, and more. It was a transformational personal development program like no other. My belief system had changed. I finally loved myself. I finally knew what I wanted. I finally knew that I am not a failure. I felt like I was enough for the first time in my life.

The program encouraged you to continue to move towards your dream life. Using the Lifebook I had created for myself, I continued stepping into each area of my life. I kept reminding myself how important all the areas of my life were. I focused on all twelve categories, striving towards the vision I had created for myself. I continued to transform. I kept reading, listening, and learning. I kept expanding my meditation so that I could go deeper. I even began to connect with my higher source, and created a definition of spirituality that felt right to me.

Looking back at my journey, I am amazed. I realize just how incredible my life has become, how important the changes I have made have been. As I reflected, I thought about how many synchronicities there had been. It made me happy to know how far I had come and how many lucky breaks had come my way. As I've stepped fully into this miraculous journey, every day, I've been given the gift of receiving not what I want, but what I need. This was perhaps the hardest lesson to learn, but I am learning it.

Taking this journey of self discovery, I have learned the importance of taking personal responsibility for my own life. I now realize that it was me that had created much of the pain and suffering in my past through the thoughts, decisions, actions, and results I had chosen. My decisions and choices were mine. The emotions I had bottled up were mine too. Now that I knew I was responsible, I could fix the issues I had in my life. It was empowering to realize that although I had created the issues in my life, that also meant that I could fix them. This was what set me free. And I have seen amazing results from living this way.

I mentioned before how I wrote my life stories and worked my way through all of my emotions. It took me a full year. I created recipes to manage all my key emotions. I even went on to author a book in the hope it would help others. I doubted my abilities to publish the book. My inner resistance became overwhelming. I even went as far as to stand in the garden and ask my departed mum if publishing the book was the right thing to do. I was confident at speaking aloud to my mum at least, and had learnt to let my brain hear what I needed to know too. I was with my husband having a much needed trip to a nearby coastal town. As we walked along the promenade, there were market stalls selling all sorts of items. One stall had four books standing on their spines, with words visible on the outside edge of the pages. I'd seen books like it before. As we walked by, the book in the middle stood out, its words were so clear. They said, "Get on with it." I truly felt like I had the biggest message ever. What I was doing was the right thing. "Thank you, mum."

My belief in something greater became just that. I did get on with it, and with that I stepped into a whole new journey. I got to understand that our perceived failures are simply challenges we are given to learn more and grow. If we don't, we die. I had not only stopped learning, but had never even taken the time to learn what I needed for me to be the healthiest version of myself. I finally realized that I could learn tools and techniques to help me be healthy in all ways. For me to be healthy in my mind, my body, and my soul. Taking responsibility for myself and finding confidence in my abilities was a monumental moment for me. Having belief in myself is so fundamental to living an incredible life, and yet my true self had been damaged and lost from an early age.

The more I learned, the more I wanted to learn. I took my learning to the next level and I uncovered beliefs that were far deeper than I could ever have imagined. At first, I had absolutely no memory of many of the experiences that had even created these beliefs. It was not because I had a poor memory, but because my subconscious mind was protecting me. Uncovering and reliving the experiences was intensely emotional, but the freedom and lightness it gave to my life was worth that moment of pain. I got to uncover what was creating such incredible resistance and prevented me from moving forward in the critical areas of my life.

Most emotional of all was uncovering the genesis of the "I'm Stupid" concept that I repeated to myself so much in life. The moment I uncovered this memory was surreal. I'd always believed it was something my father had said in my younger years. I'd not been clever and struggled at school. How wrong I was. The belief got created when I was just 18 months old. I'd fallen, fractured my skull, and was briefly unconscious. The person who found me had most likely said, "I am so stupid. It's all my fault." My subconscious mind took the belief on as its own. I'm not stupid anymore. I feel accomplished in having learnt the skills to help myself and become certified so I can help others too.

I'm taking my meditative practices to a much deeper level, learning how to shift my vibration and tune into the divine consistently. Just a short while ago, I went to bed earlier than usual. I had no idea why, but it felt right. I went to my bedroom window and could see the almost full moon, shining so brilliantly and lighting up the night sky. As I glanced, I could see the moon moving. What? My immediate thought was I must be hallucinating, so I checked my vision inside my bedroom. Was anything moving? No, all was stable. I opened the window wider and stared. The moon was moving, but not only that I could see a face. Wow! This was unbelievable. I flashed to all those times I had heard about the man on the moon. I had learned about that in my childhood, but what I was looking at was a lot more than what I had imagined.

The whole moon was covered by this face. I focussed hard and realized I could see the moon man's lips were moving. Was he talking to me? Or singing? I felt no shock or fear. I could see the lips moving but couldn't hear the words. I asked the face aloud, "What are you trying to say to me?" No matter how much I tried to understand, I couldn't. Eventually, I had to stop looking at the face on the moon, accepting that I had seen enough of whatever was going on. The next night I saw the face again, only this time on a moon that was still. The lips were moving but still I couldn't hear. I thanked the moon for whatever it was trying to tell me and immediately received its message. "Focus your learning on how to hear. Not through sound, but through vibration." Yes of course, that's why the moon was moving. It was showing me the way.

On both nights, having the window wide open and leaning out to see the grander picture, gave me time to breathe in the richness of the air. Appreciate the warmth and coolness of the oxygen that filled my lungs. Had I spent a moment longer, what flavors and bouquets would I have experienced? How else can I learn to savor the tastes of nature and smell its wondrous bouquet if I don't give myself a moment?

The way I felt on both nights has remained within me. I saw the moon again the next night. Incomplete, but the face was there for me to see. Its lips were still moving. I feel its continual desire to remind me of its message. "One day soon, dear moon, when I've mastered collapsing time and space, I'll be able to give you a direct thank you kiss."

I have completed countless courses and I have read tons of life changing books. I have learnt more about myself in the last four years than the 58 years that went before. And you know what? I like myself. Finally, I have looked back on my childhood and given myself some grace. My struggle at school wasn't because of me. I wasn't stupid. There was nothing wrong with me. I just needed to learn how to learn. My way.

I deeply appreciate everything that has happened in my journey through life. One of my favorite wisdom teachers always says that when something happens just say to yourself, "Good Thing. Bad Thing. Who knows!" This has helped me to stop judging each thing that happens and to allow the universe to work its magic in my life. I am open to whatever comes next, knowing it's what I need right now. What I want will come when the divine knows I am ready. I trust my intuition, and my soul, increasingly to discern what feels right for me.

Have I and will I make the right choices every time? Yes, because I now know what doesn't work for me, what doesn't serve me. Now, no matter what challenge I am faced with, I ask myself "What am I to learn from this?" I won't ever stop learning because learning never stops. Thanks to all I have learned, I now have, in my tried and tested toolkit ways to overcome overwhelm, have freedom from burnout, explore and transform beliefs, understand emotions, and create recipes to manage them. I have faith in my future vision, I create goals, I take action, and achieve results. I am able to move out of my comfort zone and get unstuck, with a lifestyle methodology to keep me on track. I get to use my tools whenever I need to, and I also have been blessed to have met and connected with thousands of people around the globe, sharing, learning, coaching, guiding, and listening. I have the privilege of watching people learn, grow, and flourish, all the while doing so too.

> *The greatest gift you can give a person is to wake them*
> *up to remind them of who they really are.*
> ~Neale Donald Walsch.

A message to my soul: Thank you, dear soul. I'm fully awake now. You have lifted my consciousness. I know miracles do happen. I just had to decide what I wanted them to be, and then I had to learn to have the courage to ask for the miracles to happen. I continue to learn and grow, and I'm fine tuning my antennae so I can continually step into the slipstream of this benevolent universe. My whole body is alive with the energy I feel. It's a feeling I cannot fully describe, but know it's the feeling of my Bliss

Full Future. I have complete faith in allowing you, dear soul, to guide me as you are connected to the divine source. I know it will be exciting and memorable. I now know who I truly am.

About the Author

Heidi worked for over 36 years in a corporate career. She loved her work, but had to retire early through ill health as a result of being burnt out. She was facing a future of disability, but a series of amazing events occurred and instead of disability, she went on to live a life of healing, and now envisions a glorious life for herself. Throughout her incredible journey she undertook the most robust and life changing personal development courses, culminating in healing herself, eliminating both diabetes and fibromyalgia. She has overcome a lifetime of negative emotion and limiting beliefs. This fuelled her desire and passion to connect with people around the globe, and help them find their own freedom, with a wonderful vision for their future.

Heidi shares her learning and skills through being an author, a certified emotion and belief clearing coach, a Lifebook Leader and a Mindvalley Ambassador. She is the founder of *It's Time To*, and most recently co-founder of *Inner Freedom Outer Vision*. Heidi is on a mission to be and do more, using her past, present, and learning anew to help others.

Her mission is to help people live their best life so that we can create a world full of amazing people who are transforming themselves every day. I can't wait to help you.

Author Contact Information

Email: heidi.tyler@btopenworld.com

Health is not valued until sickness comes.

-Thomas Fuller

From Paralyzed to Unstoppable

by Natasha Quariab

A diagnosis is just a speed bump
it does not determine the trajectory
or quality of your life.

~Natasha Quariab

t was the beginning of December 2021, I was on holiday in the north of Switzerland, in a little village called Gavil to be exact. I was excited as the area was beautiful and I had a lot of plans to explore from the cozy cottage that I rented on Airbnb. I had brought my art supplies with me as I had also planned on painting my Christmas cards in the evenings after enjoying some home cooked food. The cottage had a well equipped kitchen, and the fresh produce available in the area was delicious.

On my first day there I went to St Gallen, a town nearby where I worked online from a small cafe and then explored the streets, shops, christmas market, and soaked in the ambiance of the place. Everywhere was decorated for Christmas, and it was so pretty with all the twinkling lights and festive decorations. It started snowing, which just added to the magic of the place.

The next day was a little quieter. I stayed in the cottage enjoying the quiet and all the breathtaking nature around me. The snow from the day before had covered all the trees with a light sprinkling of snow, it was magical. I spent the day sipping tea and watching very talkative birds fly from branch to branch in the garden.

In the late afternoon I decided to walk to the village square, as the local shop was there and I wanted to buy a few things to cook. On the way there I noticed my right leg felt heavier than usual. I put it down to recovering from the journey and possibly overdoing it the day before. The walk to the shop and back was grueling, but I made it and congratulated myself on the achievement. That night I prayed my prayers, and went to bed expecting to be fine in the morning after a good night's sleep.

The next morning however, I woke up to find my right leg completely paralyzed. I couldn't even move my toes. I was shocked! This had happened to me before while on a life coaching retreat in Turkey in 2017, and though the paralysis didn't stop me from completing the week-long retreat, it did cause me pain. I remembered how after the week-long coaching retreat in Turkey, I had continued on to Konya for a few days and then headed to Paris to visit friends, but throughout that trip my pain kept getting worse. Eventually, I had to get an intravenous cortisone drip, and it took me about three weeks before I was able to walk again.

The difference between 2017 and this time in Switzerland was while I was in Turkey I was surrounded by my best friend Allison and nine other awesome women who were there to support me and help me when I needed help, while when I was in Paris my friends rented a wheelchair for me and pushed me around the city so that I could see everything I wanted to see. During that trip I also had access to a doctor who was able to begin cortisone therapy immediately while I was in the village of Alicate, with the help of Sabahat the owner of the charming boutique hotel I was staying at. So I had a lot of support and help to address the health scare.

In Switzerland however, even though I had travel insurance in case I got sick, getting access to cortisone without expensive tests was going to be impossible, and doing the tests was going to be exhausting and very time consuming. Heading home was not an option, as I was not going to let illness ruin my holiday. I am stubborn like that!

A quick background, I developed Multiple Sclerosis (MS) in 2002 and have had various flare ups over the years affecting different parts of my body, balance, eyesight, taste, sensation, and various other areas. I always used cortisone to reverse the flare ups and was not placed on any disease modifying drugs, though I was approved for them in 2015. My application mysteriously disappeared after I asked the senior doctor in charge too many questions which he was unable to answer during my hearing. I was never quite sure what happened, but I was not placed on any MS drugs at that time. I was, however, placed on drugs to reduce the hypersensitivity I had in my body.

In 2018 I discovered that there were many side effects to the medication I was given to reduce the hypersensitivity I was experiencing down the right side of my body. I found out that the drug killed brain cells and stopped the brain from regenerating. To say I was devastated was an understatement! I immediately threw the medication away, and spent weeks crying and praying.

I felt strongly that I could heal my body, but I didn't know how. It was at this exact time that I found Rapid Transformational Therapy by Marisa Peer. It was a course that helped you to rewire your brain, which could eventually reverse illness in the body. I signed up and eagerly applied myself to all the lessons and before I knew it, I started to feel better with zero medication. After finishing the course, I wanted to help others with this amazing healing technique that required no drugs, so I started seeing clients and helping them with all sorts of things, including losing weight, quitting smoking, overcoming phobias, improving confidence, removing money blocks, unexplained infertility, and autoimmune diseases. If a client came to me and said, "I am not going to take any medication, help me fix this!" I knew that it was possible, it just might take some time and a lot of focus, but I believed it was definitely possible. And the results proved this to be true.

My success with my patients reminded me that I could help others heal, and I could also help myself heal. When I started having this heaviness in my leg, I decided to treat myself like I would one of my clients with an autoimmune issue. The current issue for me was the time constraint, the big question was not could I heal, but rather could I reverse the paralysis with no cortisone in time for me to explore Zurich in ten days time? And would I be well enough to fly home two weeks later? The last thing I wanted was to go home in a wheelchair like I did after the Turkey trip.

I knew that Rapid Transformational Therapy (RTT) and hypnosis were powerful tools, and I decided to combine them with other tools and knowledge I had picked up since I started thinking outside the box and taking control of my health. My thought was if each of these tools is proven to work on their own, could combining them get me the results I wanted faster?

I was staying at the cottage in Gavil for another week before heading to an apartment in St Gallen. I had internet access and the very kind owners of the cottage lived next door. I called them and explained my situation as well as my plan of action. Thankfully both Andreas and Barbara were "dream masters" who held workshops and trainings that taught people skills like lucid dreaming, and were very into alternative ways of healing, so they didn't think my plan was too out of the ordinary and offered me lots of support.

My idea was to take care of all the different elements that made up a healthy body. This meant focusing on the physical, the mental, and the energetic bodies. I approached it by focusing first on the foods I was eating to improve my physical health. Then, I rewired my brain with a type of hypnosis called Rapid Transformational Therapy (RTT) as well as visualization. Then, I healed my energetic body by using a technique called Energy Medicine. I will go through each one of these with you now.

Physical Body: Nutrition

Step one in serving the physical part of the puzzle was to make sure I had the nutrition needed to rebuild the damaged nerves. I went online and researched what nutrients I would need to build nerves and where I could find them in food. I didn't take any supplements, I wanted to get all my nutrients through the food I was eating. I asked Andreas if he could drive me to a supermarket where I could buy blueberries and some green leafy vegetables. Holding on to the supermarket trolley for dear life, I managed to hobble around the store and get everything I thought I would need. I filled my cart with brussel sprouts, spinach, blueberries, and some other green leafy vegetables native to the area that Andreas assured me were full of nutrients and would be very good for me. The second component was to stop eating any food that might be causing inflammation. I decided to cut out dairy, gluten, and seed oil.

Once I got home I noticed that my right arm was also feeling super weak, meaning the paralysis was all down my right side. This was even worse than Turkey, but I tried not to panic and just told myself that it would make for a better story once everything was overcome. I decided it was time to rewire my brain.

Rewiring the Mind: Hypnosis & Visualization

Once I had gotten my physical needs met by ensuring I was adding in healthy foods that would supply me with all the nutrients I needed and I had eliminated the foods that would cause inflammation in my body, I turned to rewire my mind. In recent years, there has been tremendous research on the brain which shows that the brain can actually change and rewire itself depending on the thoughts you have in your head. This is a very exciting field which has shown us that the brain is, indeed, an amazingly complex mechanism that we are just starting to learn about. I knew I could use my brain to move towards abundant health, and I decided to use hypnosis and visualization to do this.

Hypnosis

During this recent health problem, I had tried self hypnosis on myself, but didn't feel like I had gotten to the root cause of my issue. Sometimes it is hard for the mind that created the issue to listen to reason from the same mind trying to heal things. I understood that I needed someone who wasn't me to work with me, so I called my friend Sandra, who had also completed the course on Rapid Transformational Therapy. She immediately did a session on me and together we identified the thoughts that were causing the malfunction and upgraded them. It worked miracles. Sandra made me a great hypnotic recording that I began listening to that day and every day after that as I healed.

I was starting to feel a bit better. Standing in one spot was alright for me, but in order to move around the house I needed to hold on to things and drag my right leg. Getting to the bathroom was a bit of a problem as it was on the floor above me, but luckily there was a small toilet downstairs so I didn't need to go up the stairs every time I needed to use the facilities. I did however need to make it upstairs to go to bed, brush my teeth, and shower. The climb was a very slow process, but I kept telling myself what an awesome story this would be one day.

Visualization

During the entire process, I continually told myself that I would get better. I would visualize myself being active and fully healthy. I spent time each day actually picturing myself healed and whole. This technique is called visualization, which I believe was crucial for me in my healing journey.

Visualizing your goal and being able to see yourself well is quite possibly the most powerful thing you can do to promote healing. I kept seeing myself walking, running, and standing on stage, inspiring other people to heal. I knew there had to be a higher purpose for the suffering I was going through. I have always believed that there is a reason for everything, and I decided my reason was to learn how to overcome this illness so that I could teach other people how to heal themselves as well. I knew that this was important information to get to people because nobody had ever told me that healing was possible without medication, yet here I was doing it. I wanted to bring this news to others.

You see, in the past I was able to reverse my flare ups using cortisone, however, the side effects that I experienced while taking the drug and once I stopped were quite awful. From the metallic taste in my mouth to the aches and pain all over my body, the side effects were quite severe. Often the side effects were much more painful than the flare up itself. I knew this was true for me, and figured it was probably true for other people as well.

What I liked about the alternative practices I was experimenting with was that there were no side effects with any of them. If one of the methods doesn't help you, at least they didn't harm you as the medications did. Visualization is one such technique that can be used for a multitude of things, including healing. When you visualize something, your brain sees it as really happening, which is why it works. Between the hypnosis and the visualization, I noticed my mind was getting stronger and stronger. Now that I had dealt with my physical body, it was time to heal my energetic body.

Healing the Energetic Body

After visualization, nutrition, and rapid transformational therapy, my next step was energy medicine, so I asked Andreas and Barbara if there were any energy healers in the village. They informed me that there was one they knew of that usually worked with animals but didn't speak much English. I laughed and said that I doubt cows and horses speak German but he still manages to help them. The healer arrived the next day. He was amazing and was able to balance out my energy. He told me that he felt the issue stemmed from my head area. This confirmed my thought that the issue I was suffering from was a result of a thought.

You see thoughts create feelings, and while thoughts are the language of the mind, feelings are the language of the body. So I had had a thought which had generated a feeling which had made my body react the way that it did. Crazy! Right?

Now I figured that though I was listening to the hypnotic recording to upgrade the thought and I understood what the thought behind the paralysis was, by using rapid transformational therapy I needed to speed things up by reasserting my mind's dominance over my body. The body is meant to be controlled by the mind. This is generally the rule, but sometimes the body goes rouge and thinks it can do what it likes. The body continues running on old programming (in this case the original thought that created the issue), until we change it. I determined that for me, the best way to reassert dominance would be through meditation.

Using meditation the body is conditioned to go back to the default setting of being controlled by the mind. I wanted my body to do what it was being told to do in the hypnotic recording, and though listening to the recording over time would make that happen, I didn't really have time for my body to take its sweet time. Instead I needed fast results! It was time to get serious with my mediation.

That evening I signed up to a meditation programme with Dr. Joe Dispenza and I started learning how to meditate. Before signing up, I searched for stories of people who had overcome paralysis using Dr. Joe's meditations, and there were many. The fact that they had done it was proof that I could too. Up until that point I knew meditation was powerful, but never felt the need to dive into it too deeply. That evening and for the next week I poured all of my energy into meditating, doing it three or four times a day, paired with the hypnotic recording, nutritious food, and constant visualization. I was a woman on a mission!

The deep dive into learning everything I could about meditation gave my mind something to focus on, almost like a chew toy. It was so busy learning that it didn't have time to dwell on negative thoughts like, "What if this doesn't work?", "What if I never walk again?" or "What if all this is all just wishful thinking?" This was a good thing, as negative thoughts would not serve me during this healing time. I was running out of time and there was no room for anything that wasn't serving me.

The fact that there was a huge snow storm the day after my supermarket trip relieved me of any fear of missing out that I might have otherwise had, as there was no way for me to go anywhere even if I wanted to! Apart from looking out the window every now and again to admire the snow, the focus was healing.

Healing at Last!

A week after working on my self-healing, I was able to lift my right leg a little, and wriggle my big toe. This might not seem like a lot but to me, it was huge. I still couldn't control my right hand much. My attempt at painting a christmas card for Andreas and Barbara the night before ended in splotches of paint on a card and child-like writing inside, definitely not my best work! But the progress with my leg buoyed my spirits and gave me hope.

Everyday after the week had passed there was improvement, I was delighted at the progress, it meant what I was doing was working. By now I had moved to the apartment in St Gallen. I was determined to see a little of Switzerland before the holiday was over, so I booked a panoramic train from St Gallen to Lucerne and back. I also decided I was going to walk the 13 minutes to the station. It was challenging, and I had to periodically stop and hold onto the poles and railings on the way, but I made it! It took me a bit longer than it should have, but I made it! I celebrated by getting my eye makeup done at the cosmetic shop in the station.

The next day I went to Zurich early in the morning, I spent the day walking around the city (technically walking from sit down spot to sit down spot) but I was so happy as I couldn't have done this a mere ten days ago. The trip went well and I was walking a lot! It was a huge achievement. I continued to improve and by the time I made it back home to Amman, Jordan, I was walking almost normally.

The whole experience made me realize how powerful the human body is, and that self healing is possible even when dealing with something that all the doctors say is incurable. I understood that no one had ever taught me how to heal, and if they had I could have avoided a lot of pain and suffering. I couldn't understand how everyone wasn't taught how to help their bodies heal, and I vowed to make it my life's mission to teach anyone who was willing to learn how to heal naturally.

Since returning home in December 2021, I have given lectures and workshops on how to self heal and even created an online course with a step by step guide. I have expanded my healing tools and I now teach people to focus on 14 things in order to live healthy. I list these below.

14 Steps to Healing Naturally

1. Visualization
2. Nutrition
3. Thoughts
4. Energy
5. Meditation
6. Movement
7. Novelty
8. Sunshine
9. Emotions
10. Fasting
11. Toxins
12. Sleep
13. Breath
14. Blessings and intention

Final Words

In my opinion no one should ever be sick, a disease is exactly that it is a dis-ease, it is a message from our body that things are not in balance. Listening to our bodies when we exhibit symptoms or have a disease is essential. Once we identify why the body is doing what it is doing, we are able to give the body what it needs to heal, and in this way, everything can be fixed.

No matter what you are currently going through, know that it will pass and an amazing healthy life awaits you, learn what you need to do to heal and then do the work. I am living proof that anything is possible. I am grateful for my journey because I now have a deeper life's mission to help others heal naturally.

With love,
Natasha

About the Author

---✦---

Natasha is an international inspirational speaker, a serial entrepreneur, hypnotherapist, and transformation coach. She helps her clients overcome whatever is stopping them from living their best life. Over the years she has helped people with weight issues, love blocks, money blocks, broken hearts, grief, phobias, depression, anxiety, confidence issues, stopping smoking, and autoimmune illnesses. Nothing stops her, and she teaches her clients how to be unstoppable too! Natasha believes the journey to a great life doesn't need to be hard and should be as pleasurable as possible, as the journey is just as important as the destination. She lives in Amman, Jordan and serves people from around the world with her online courses and 1:1 sessions. When she isn't serving her clients you can find her in the garden enjoying the many days of sunshine Jordan is blessed with.

Author Contact Information

---✦---

Email: Natasha.Quariab@gmail.com
Websites: www.HypnotherapyME.com
           www.NatashaTalks.com

*Wellness is the complete
integration of body mind and spirit.*

~Greg Anderson

My Journey

by Dr. Anurag Vats

*Out of suffering have emerged the strongest souls;
the most massive characters are seared with scars.*

~Khalil Gibran

I am going to share the insights of the most significant decade of my life where I had the most profound physical and mental transformation as a human being. This chapter contains some remarkable events that at the time felt like they were failures of mine, however, in hindsight, I realize that these events were part of the process of growing up as a conscious being. They were not pleasant experiences, and they shook me a lot, however, those failures made me who I am now and I am grateful for everything and everyone that was part of the journey.

While growing up, the concept of health was a simple idea of not falling sick and whenever you do get sick, how fast you could recover. In my childhood, my family made a lot of home cooked meals, and like any household, food was associated with happy occasions as well as emotions. I have grown up my whole life believing that food cooked at home was healthier, irrespective of what was being cooked. There was a noticeable shift in our attitude about eating as the notion of western fast food was spreading through cities. Pizza burger joints came into prominence, and there was a noticeable shift in what we were eating. I don't exactly remember when it became more frequent that junk food was a commonality at home, however, we gradually shifted to a less healthy diet of processed foods. Eventually, I hit rock bottom when I was afflicted with jaundice. It happened during my high school final exams which resulted in me taking a two month break from school to rest and recover.

This impacted me significantly as it affected my exam preparation and general health. Once I got better, it was back to my studies and before I knew it, I was off to college. I was being careful while eating out, yet I started facing issues with digestion and often had heartburn and had episodes of G.E.R.D as well. These were intense years for me, as academics took over everything else.

Eventually, the stress affected me and as my entire life began to revolve around my studies, it eventually affected my eating habits. I began to eat a lot of processed foods again and this took a toll on my appearance, health, and fitness levels. I didn't even realize how unhealthy I was getting until the pandemic came and we went into full lock down. I went to the doctor and he told me that I needed to take care of my health and although I did try the gym and several forms of dieting, I always ended up either getting injured or getting a digestive issue which caused me to cease my efforts.

Nothing was working for me, so I continued to search for answers until I eventually found a holistic framework for health, and that is when I began to see my entire life turning around. I was getting healthier and happier and my energy levels were stellar.

My journey has been one filled with many ups and downs. During the lockdown period, I realized that I had not been taking care of myself. My search for a holistic way of approaching my health has been filled with every emotion. Now, I am healthier than I have ever been and that is why I have chosen to share this framework with you. I know it will help you become the healthiest version of yourself.

The Holistic Framework for Health

I realized during my health journey that many of the contemporary healing modalities were basically a transformation of the various healing practices from around the world dating way back to 5,000 years ago. So I dove in and learned all I did about these ancient practices and created this framework.

The holistic framework is based on the laws of nature, It emphasizes the connection of mind, body, and spirit. The goal is to achieve maximum well-being, where everything is functioning the very best that is possible. Using this framework, each person must accept responsibility for their own level of well-being, and their everyday choices. It's not just about being fit physically, it's about being fit in all aspects of health including mental fitness, emotional well being, behavioral health, and even spiritual health. This framework recognizes that we are multidimensional beings, and we must take all of these areas into account because when one part is not working at its best, it impacts all the other parts. Everything is indeed connected.

I was amazed as I researched different aspects of health because it all echoed the Ayurvedic lifestyle that I had learned about in my youth. Ayurveda takes the person as a whole and examines how a person interacts with their respective environment. In Ayurveda, they have a concept called tridosha, which literally means "faults or disease." The tridoshas are the three forces of the body, which creates a balance in health and produces ailments when it is out of equilibrium. The three doshas are Vata, Pitta, and Kapha.

The Vata assures that the body movements take place without obstructions. This includes absorption, cell ion exchange, nervous system conduction, all types of excretions, breathing, and musculoskeletal functions.

The Pitta has a role that brings transformation and it acts as the heat energy that assists in digesting food at gross and cellular levels. It imparts warmth, vision, and color to the body.

The Kapha force makes the body stable, the structures well held with muscle, tendons, ligaments, and fats. It also forms the protective coverings and fluid shock absorber for joints, brain (CSF), and spinal cord.

So the basic idea is to live an extraordinary life and in order to do that, we must make the correct choices so that we can lead meaningful lives. We must address all areas of our life in order to have the energy levels we need to live the amazing life we desire.

The tools I used that helped me immensely were paying close attention to my food choices and opting to cook my own food from wholesome ingredients as much as possible. I created a schedule for eating so that I wouldn't ever get hungry, so that I could keep to my healthy diet. I removed all forms of processed foods and sugar from my diet and I saw a massive improvement in my body as well as my emotional state when I did that. I felt my mind getting clearer and clearer as I changed my diet.

I focused on drinking lots of water, and I found that staying hydrated helps me feel great all day long. Being hydrated also has the added benefit of making me feel less hungry throughout the day.

One of the biggest changes was that I created a sleep schedule and stuck with it. I reduced the use of electronics and screens in the hours leading to bed, which helped me to sleep deeper and wake up much more refreshed. This one change alone is one that totally changed my life, and I think that it could change yours as well.

I decided to educate myself and started reading non-academic books to increase my knowledge about all aspects of health. These books gave me great ideas on how I could change my habits to create a healthier lifestyle.

During the pandemic, I was lucky to get involved with an online community and I began to have like minded friends from around the world.

This has worked wonders for me and has given me the accountability I always needed. These new friends were a source of support, but also inspiration, and I feel truly blessed to have them in my life. Building a network of people who are interested in the same things as you can totally and utterly change you and change your outlook. I know because it certainly changed mine.

As I mentioned earlier, we want to address wellbeing in all the dimensions of life. We are each unique individuals so it is essential to find out the areas of life that are important to you for you to become the healthiest person you can be. As you dive deep into who you are and what you want, it is important to consider your deeper inner life. Some call this consciousness, others call it the soul. Whatever you call it, this deeper inner you must be addressed as you embark upon your own health journey.

There are thousands of inscriptions from different centuries and almost every one of them talks about awakening consciousness. It has been a topic thought about by humankind since the dawn of time. I realized that in order to be totally healthy, I had to address this area of my life that I had ignored for so long. So now, I am working on awakening my consciousness and allowing my mind, body, and soul to create an equilibrium. It is a work in progress, but I am going to achieve it. I have faith in myself, but I also have faith in you because if I can do it, you can do it too.

We live in a time where all the information we could ever need is at our fingertips. We no longer need to move towards the mountains to search for it by ourselves, it's all in the palm of our hands, in our cellphones. Regardless of where you are, have faith that you can turn it around and take any obstacle as a lesson.,

My failure taught me that what I wanted to become and what I was seeking were separate entities and just by understanding that, I am able to live fully rather than just being alive. So begin now to study wellness. Whether it is Ayurveda or Yoga or Holistic practices or any other ways to heal, recover, or rejuvenate, the important thing is the decision to go on the journey. The real healing starts within ourselves first, and that is most important to acknowledge. Looking within and becoming more present allows us to live in a sustainable way, and just imagine that if our generation embraces the transformation, the coming generation automatically shall be transformed, and this shall give our planet a better stand in future. And isn't that an amazing vision to look towards?

In closing, I want to encourage you to look deep within and be totally and completely honest about where you are physically, mentally, emotionally, and spiritually. Take stock of where you are, and then begin to educate yourself as I did. Perhaps my story can give you a blueprint to follow and soon enough, you too will be living a healthier life. I wish you health and happiness as you move towards the healthiest version of you.

With love,
Anurag

About the Author

Dr. Anurag Vats is an Oral & Maxillofacial surgeon in India by profession and an entrepreneur at heart. He is an aspiring author and wishes to work with people by educating and promoting holistic lifestyle. He aims to work with the communities around the world to develop sustainable living and build a better future.

Final Words

Dear Reader,

As you've journeyed through these pages, you've witnessed the remarkable power of the human spirit—the resilience that lies within each of us, waiting to be awakened. These stories, shared straight from the hearts of those who have faced their darkest hours, stand as testaments to the truth that within every challenge lies an opportunity for transformation.

Life's twists and turns often lead us to unexpected places, places we never thought we'd find ourselves. These moments—the ones that shake us to our core, leaving us vulnerable and uncertain—are what we refer to as the "dark moments of the soul." It's in these moments that we come face to face with our own vulnerabilities, fears, and limitations.

But it's also in these moments that we have a choice—a choice to remain in the shadows or to rise, even stronger than before. The authors of these stories have made that choice, and their experiences illuminate a path for all of us. They remind us that adversity is not the end of the road; it's the beginning of a new journey.

Every tale you've read showcases a different facet of the human experience, yet they all share a common thread—the willingness to confront their demons and use their pain as a catalyst for growth. These stories show us that the very difficulties that once seemed insurmountable can become the fuel for remarkable change.

In the heart of darkness, we find the seeds of transformation. Just as a flower pushes through the cracks in the pavement to reach the sun, so too can we rise from the challenges that threaten to hold us down. The road may be difficult, but it's in the struggle that we discover our true strength.

And so, dear reader, I invite you to reflect on these stories and recognize the potential that resides within you. Each one of us is capable of creating the life of our dreams, of becoming the most extraordinary version of ourselves. It starts with acknowledging that the journey will have its hardships, but it's these very hardships that will shape us into the individuals we're meant to be.

Remember, transformation is not a one-time event; it's a continuous journey. Embrace the darkness, for it's where the stars shine the brightest. Embrace the challenges, for they are the stepping stones to your greatness. Embrace your story, for it's uniquely yours, and it has the power to inspire and uplift others.

You are the author of your own narrative. Your past does not define you; it refines you. Your trials do not limit you; they propel you forward. With courage, determination, and a belief in the boundless potential within you, there's no limit to what you can achieve.

So go forth, write your story, and let your transformation be a testament to the incredible journey that is life.

With unwavering faith in your journey,
Kerry and Lawrence

Be Extraordinary Publishing

Check out all the books under the Be Extraordinary imprint. Our mission is to show you how to be the very best version of yourself, how to live the very best life you can possibly live. Our books are all about bringing attention to all the important areas of your life so that you can uplevel them all.

We publish books on a variety of health and wellness topics as well as on peak performance and mindset. We focus on personal transformation and teach you how you can live your best life. Look for books on a wide variety of topics including nutrition, exercise, yoga, pilates, meditation, breathwork, mindfulness practices, and self care. Our books will show you how you can upgrade your life using simple techniques, tips and tricks to create a magnificent life.

We also bring you stories of the heroes amongst us. Stories of the journey towards extraordinary living. These books illuminate how every person is on a Hero's Journey, how every person is on a journey towards extraordinary. Look for our books on Amazon, in bookstores and everywhere books are sold.

Please visit our website
beextraordiinarypublishing.com

Excellence is doing ordinary things extraordinarily well.

~John W. Gardner

Look for Other Books from Be Extraordinary Publishing

Total Health for Extraordinary Living

Are you ready to have total health and wellness? If so, this book is for you! *Total Health for Extraordinary Living* is filled with tips and techniques for living a healthy, happy lifestyle. With contributions from 30 coaches, peak performers, athletes and weekend warriors, you will find everything you need to live at peak health in this book.

These are the stories of people who had amazing health transformations. They are sharing their stories to show you that it is never too late to move towards the expansive health and endless energy that is your natural state of being.

Total Health For Extraordinary Living encourages you to look at your health holistically. This means that you are paying attention to your physical body by eating right and exercising but it also means taking care of your mental health as well as your spiritual side. Holistic health means body, mind and spirit are all working in unison. This book will cover many different aspects of health so that you can create a healthy lifestyle and ensure total health for your entire lifetime. You will learn:

- How to implement a simple exercise program for ultra fitness
- How to create a diet that nourishes you.
- How to use affirmations to improve your self image.
- How to use a simple exercise each morning to change your mindset.
- How running can become a meditation.

- How to add meditation to your schedule.
- How adding gratitude practice can uplevel your life.
- How nurturing community can help you live the healthy lifestyle you imagine.
- Learn to make health an everyday part of your life.
- Learn how gratitude can change your life.

You will learn how to take care of your physical body as well as to learn mindfulness techniques and health techniques that will help you live in peak health. Check out this book today so that you can begin down the road to total health!

The Extraordinary Living Series

The Extraordinary Living Series is a series of books with one central premise. You can live the life of your dreams, you can become the person you dream of becoming. All it takes is action. The series teaches you the tools, techniques and tips that will help you take control of your life so that you can create the masterpiece life you have always imagined.

Tools for Extraordinary Living: The Snooze Button Sessions: Book 1 in the Extraordinary Living Series

Tools for Extraordinary Living: The Snooze Button Sessions is the first book in the Extraordinary Living Series. This is the book that started it all. The Snooze Button Technique was born out of an epiphany Kerry Fisher had one day while hiking with her family. She came into a clearing in the woods and suddenly flashed back to a scene from her youth where she had been in a similar clearing writing down all her hopes and dreams for her future. As the adult Kerry remembered what the young Kerry had written, she realized all her dreams had come true. Which was great. Except for one thing, she still wasn't happy.

This revelation set Kerry on a journey of personal growth and transformation which completely changed her life, her family's life and the direction of her career. You see, Kerry had discovered that we all know what we have to do to have an incredible life, we just don't know how to do it. So Kerry created the Snooze Button Technique to give people a way to take action immediately. She began to share this technique with her family, her student, her family and the results were incredible. Soon enough, people were reporting that they were changing, their life was changing. The results were so incredible that Kerry knew she had to share this technique with the world so she wrote this book to do just that. If you are ready to create change in your life, get the book today. It is filled with simple, nourishing practices that will supercharge your life.

Routines for Extraordinary Living
A Manual for Life
Book 2 in The Extraordinary Living Series

The second book in the extraordinary living series, *Routines for Extraordinary Living* is for those people who want to create change in their life but don't know where to start. The book takes you step by step through your day, teaching you how to establish nourishing routines throughout the day to move you towards the extraordinary life you deserve. This book is all about creating a lifestyle where healthy routines are woven into your day. You will create practices that are built into your everyday life that nourish your body, your mind and your spirit. Before you know it, your life will be one of ease and flow which enables you to have the energy you need to create the life you desire.

Mindset Mastery for Extraordinary Living:
Book 2 in the Extraordinary Living Series

The third book in the Extraordinary Living Series, Mindset Mastery for Extraordinary Living is for those people who are truly ready to take their

219

lives to the next level. The book goes deep into the science behind why we do what we do. You will learn about the way your brain and your nervous system work and how you can use your biology to create the life you have dreamed of. You will learn how to make goals that align with your true purpose here on earth and then you will create the plan to make those goals a reality. This book examines the way our emotions work, how our nervous system and brain seek to protect us, and gives you the tools you need to rewire your brain so that you can create the masterpiece of a life that you deserve.

The Quest for Extraordinary Living:
Insights on the Journey to Extraordinary

One of Kerry's deepest wishes from a very young age was to be a writer. It was a secret dream she rarely shared with anyone.

On January 2, 2022, Kerry was sitting in her backyard reading The Alchemist by Paulo Coelho. The book is about a shepherd boy who was on a quest to find his life's purpose. As Kerry read the book, she asked herself one simple question, "What is my life's purpose?" She was surprised when the thought immediately jumped into her head, "You are here to write."

The next thought was this, "What does a writer do?"

The answer again jumped into her head, "A writer writes."

And as the sun rose over the horizon, in those early days of 2022, Kerry made a decision that she would write every single day for an entire year. She decided to write on a platform called Insights by Mindvalley and each day for a full year, she wrote an insight. She didn't miss a day. The daily writing fueled her passion for writing and soon enough, she began writing the Extraordinary Living series.

On January 2nd, 2022, early in the day as the sun was rising, Kerry sat outside reading the Alchemist once more and then she went to write her 365th article. As she did, she began to read back through the year of insights and she realized she wanted to share these stories in book form. She began the massive task of organizing the articles by topic and created the Insights for Extraordinary Living. They are simple stories, stories of self reflection and deep soul searching. They remind us that every single person we meet can become our teacher, every single event in our life can serve as a lesson.

Check out these lovely little stories of life's lessons. They remind you that you can become the person you dream of becoming, you can live the extraordinary life you imagine.

Breathwork for Extraordinary Living

A deep dive into the breath. The mystics have been practicing breath exercises for thousands of years. They found that doing these breath exercises helped them get to deeper levels of meditation. The yogis have known the power of the breath as well. So have many of the Eastern traditions. The exciting thing is that science is now catching up with the wisdom of the ages. Recent studies have shown how powerful a breath practice can be in creating new states within your body. Indeed, the studies indicate that breath is an incredible tool we can use to help balance our emotions and our mental state. If you want to learn simple breath tools you can use to help you live a life of balance and ease, look for this wonderful book.

Meditation for Extraordinary Living

Meditation has long been used by many religious and spiritual traditions to tap into altered states of mind. The mystics from the ages used meditation to help them to move into deep states of awareness and consciousness. They found that meditation kept them calm in body, mind and spirit. Meditation has become increasingly common across the world because it is one of the best ways to change your state of being. This book will teach you many different meditation techniques so you can bring this practice into your life.

For Further Information

Thank you for reading this book. It is our hope that you received a lot of value from the material presented here. It is also our desire that this book will help you become the next greatest and healthiest version of yourself.

This is the first in a series of Total Life Transformation co-author books on Health and Holistic Living. Each book contains the stories of coaches, elite athletes, wellness educators and everyday people as they share the secrets they have discovered for living their healthiest, happiest life.

We aim to find authors who have simple tips that are easy to put into action. We believe that action is the only way to live the healthiest life. We all know what to do, the books in this series tell you how to do it.

If you enjoyed this book, please leave a review on the site where you purchased the book.

Please share this book with anyone who you think could benefit from the information in this book.

Now this is not the end.
It is not even the beginning of the end.
But it is, perhaps, the end of
the beginning.

~Winston Churchill

www.ingramcontent.com/pod-product-compliance
Lightning Source LLC
LaVergne TN
LVHW051229080426
835513LV00016B/1490